A Student's Vocabulary of Biblical Hebrew

Listed According to Frequency and Cognate

PREPARED AND ARRANGED BY

George M. Landes

Union Theological Seminary, New York

CHARLES SCRIBNER'S SONS
NEW YORK

20

PRINTED IN THE UNITED STATES OF AMERICA

ISBN   0-02-367410-5

Library of Congress Catalog Card Number 61-7224

Contents

Foreword

A major exercise for the student of any foreign language—and one that persists long after he has mastered the chief difficulties of such phenomena as script, pronunciation, grammar, and idiom—is the acquisition of a good working vocabulary. For the English student of Biblical Hebrew, the task is further complicated by the significant paucity of etymological relationships between the vocables of Hebrew and those in his own language. Moreover, not only does Hebrew writing look vastly different, but also when its words are pronounced, their sounds rarely suggest meanings in English identical with their actual definitions.

For many years, students of Biblical Hebrew who have sought a tool to facilitate their learning of vocabulary have become familiar with William R. Harper's *Hebrew Vocabularies*, first published in a private edition in 1882, and then brought out in a fifth enlarged edition by Charles Scribners' Sons in 1893. Despite its usefulness, this fifth edition was never reprinted, though a greatly abridged form of it appeared as an appendix in all editions of Harper's *Introductory Hebrew Method and Manual*, most recently (1958) brought out in a paperback edition by the University of Chicago Press. In 1956, J. Barton Payne, Professor of Old Testament at Trinity Seminary in Chicago, published his own *Hebrew Vocabularies* (copyright by Baker Book House), based upon three lists drawn from the 1893 edition of Harper's original work, to which Prof. Payne made certain additions and corrections, completely reworking the list of Hebrew Particles (Part III in his arrangement). This was followed in 1959 by John D. W. Watts' *Lists of Words Occurring Frequently in the Hebrew Bible* (copyright by E. J. Brill, Leiden, Netherlands, but distributed in America by the Wm. B. Eerdmans Publishing Co.), which utilized the same three lists of Harper selected by Payne (though somewhat further abridged), but arranged them in a more useful format, and helpfully provided stem indications, where appropriate, for the verbs. Dr. Watts also made revisions and corrections in comparison with the Köhler-Baumgartner Hebrew-Aramaic Dictionary (*Lexicon in Veteris Testamenti Libros*, Leiden, 1953).

Now both of these recent efforts to simplify, shorten, and correct Harper's *Hebrew Vocabularies* have been a welcome auxiliary to students of Biblical

Hebrew, but in the present writer's opinion, their full effectiveness has been hampered by rigidly adhering to Harper's main organizational principle, viz., listing the words alphabetically in groups of descending frequency categories (500-5,000, 300-500, 200-300, etc.), with verbs, nouns, and particles separated into three distinct lists. From a methodological and pedagogical standpoint, such an arrangement leaves something to be desired, especially when its basic intent to ease the student's burden of memorizing large numbers of Hebrew words is carefully considered. Hence the *raison d'être* for this new effort to reformulate the vocabulary lists of Biblical Hebrew.

A fundamental truism of learning theory is that we increase our knowledge by association, particularly by relating things which, by their nature, belong together. Many languages, including Hebrew, form a large number of their words from basic verbal ideas. Thus a great many of the non-verbal parts of speech—nouns, adjectives, adverbs, even prepositions and other particles—trace their derivation from verbal roots. When a student sets about to learn Hebrew verbs, he should therefore do so in conjunction with their nominal and other cognates. For when he studies a verb and its cognate(s) listed together, he often becomes aware of natural mnemonic devices which help him to remember the words so arranged. Moreover, not only is he then able to see more clearly the relationships between these words, but he is also encouraged to learn a larger number of them than would be the case were the verbs divorced from their derivatives in separate lists. As a pedagogical aid for learning vocabulary, the listing of verbs with their cognates is not new; it has been regularly followed by those who prepare printed vocabulary cards for students of various ancient and modern languages. For New Testament Greek, it has been successfully done by Bruce M. Metzger in his useful *Lexical Aids for Students of New Testament Greek* (privately printed in an enlarged edition, 1955). Even William R. Harper in section VIII of his *Hebrew Vocabularies* (1893 edition) made use of it for Biblical Hebrew, but unfortunately this section was never reprinted in subsequent editions and revisions of his work, and never has it been worked out with the comprehensiveness that this present apparatus attempts.

In the following pages the Vocabularies are

arranged in three major lists. Throughout the first two, words are grouped according to frequency *and* their cognate relationships. List I is the largest, containing every verbal root and its respective derivatives (if extant) that occur in the Hebrew Bible from about ten to over five hundred times. The English definitions have been placed in columns next to the Hebrew with sufficient space to permit the student conveniently to study and review the Hebrew without having to look directly at the English. The list is subdivided into frequency categories, much in the fashion of Harper's work. Frequency ranges are employed for all words occurring 70 or more times in the Old Testament, while words which occur less than 70 times are listed with their exact number of occurrences (all figures are based on word counts made from Solomon Mandelkern's *Veteris Testamenti Concordantiae Hebraicae atque Chaldaicae*, reprinted 1955). Verbs with an incidence of 70 or more are listed alphabetically, but those below 70 are catalogued in a descending frequency order, most often determined by the frequency of their derivatives. That is, verbs having cognates occurring more than 500 times are listed first in each of the frequency categories below 70, while verbs with cognates belonging in the 24-10 range are listed last. Obviously, this arrangement could not be pursued in detail, since a number of verbs have several cognates which vary in frequency ranges. In general, however, the position of a verb in the groups below 70 is determined by its cognate with the highest frequency figure(s). With the cognates also, only frequency ranges are specified for those appearing 70 or more times, but precise enumerations are indicated for those below 70. If a verbal root has more than one cognate, the derivatives are listed in decreasing frequency order.

List II contains every verbal root in the Old Testament with a frequency of less than ten, but which also has a cognate or cognates with a frequency of more than ten. The format of this list much resembles that of List I. Verbs are not listed alphabetically, but in accordance with the frequency of their derivatives. Exact frequencies are recorded for those derivatives occurring less than 70 times. When specific Biblical texts are cited in parentheses after the English definition of the verbal root, they denote the only occurrences of the root in the Hebrew Bible.

List III contains the common nouns and other parts of speech which occur in the Old Testament ten or more times, but which have no extant verbal cognates in the Hebrew Bible. The words are arranged alphabetically in the frequency categories above 70, in descending order in accordance with their exact frequency occurrences below 70.

Most of the English definitions are based on those given (in German) in the Köhler-Baumgartner dictionary. Only basic definitions are given.

An Appendix listing most of the Hebrew proper and place names of the Old Testament with an incidence of 70 or more is added for the convenience of beginning Hebrew students, who sometimes have difficulty with this type of word. The names are arranged in decreasing frequency order. Where such derive simply from a single verbal root, they may be found listed with that root in the appropriate vocabulary division.

Since none of the lists are consistently alphabetical in their arrangement, an Index has been provided to facilitate the rapid finding of the Hebrew words. This will be especially useful for those who merely wish to look up the cognate(s) of a certain root, or to see whether a specific word has an extant cognate or not, or to check the frequency of a particular word. Obviously the apparatus should never be used as a surrogate for the lexicon.

In learning words, the student should select from all three lists as he proceeds through the vocabularies, rather than taking each as it comes. A suggested order of learning is as follows:

1. List I A., II, nos. 1-8, III A.
2. List I B., II, nos. 9-23, III B-C.
3. List I C., II, nos. 24-38 III D.
4. List I D., II, nos. 39-47, III E.
5. List I E., II, nos. 48-63, III F.
6. List I F., II, nos. 64-101, III G.
7. List I G., II, nos. 102-192, III H.

Though the accuracy of the apparatus has been carefully checked by the author and others, a work of this kind is highly susceptible to errors and omissions, and those who use it will probably find some of both. The author will always appreciate being informed of any corrections or additions that should be made. Though I take full responsibility for all inaccuracies, I wish to express my gratitude to all those who have been helpful, in one way or another, in the preparation of the vocabularies for publication. I especially owe a debt of thanks to Prof. Prescott H. Williams, Jr., who carefully examined the preliminary mimeographed copy of the manuscript, on the basis of which he made many corrections and suggestions; to Prof. David Noel Freedman, who graciously offered the use of his own vocabulary list containing exact frequency counts, and who studied the next-to-final draft of the present work; to my students at Union Theological Seminary, particularly Mr. James Wood, who spent many hours meticulously checking most of the frequencies and making corrections where necessary, but also many others, who, as beginning students in Hebrew, have used these lists in learning Hebrew vocabulary, and as a result of their efforts, have suggested several ways of improving the original manuscript. Finally, I am grateful to my colleagues in the Old Testament Department, Profs. James A. Muilenburg and Samuel L. Terrien, for their interest and encouragement in this project.

GEORGE M. LANDES

SIGLA AND ABBREVIATIONS

1. *Sigla*

(1) A number in parentheses preceding (reading from right to left) a root, cognate, or other word, designates a particular set of definitions or meanings, among others, attached to the same sequence of consonants elsewhere in the Hebrew Bible. The numbering follows that given in the Köhler-Baumgartner lexicon.

(1)† The above symbol followed by a dagger indicates that another word having the same consonants does *not* occur in this apparatus.

* An asterisk placed before a Hebrew word indicates that the word is nowhere extant in its absolute form in the Hebrew Bible.

(?) A question-mark in parentheses following the listing of a Hebrew cognate indicates that its derivation from the root under which it is placed is uncertain.

> Indicates derivation from a root or other word.

< Indicates a word goes back to a specified root.

(13, Ex.) If only the name of an Old Testament book is indicated after a frequency figure, it means that the word occurs in that book alone.

(Hi.) When a verb has a meaning or set of meanings which are regularly (though not necessarily exclusively) expressed in one or more particular stems, these stems are noted in parentheses after the appropriate English definition(s).

(Qal) If a verb is extant only in the Qal conjugation, the word Qal in parentheses occurs before the Hebrew rendering of the root.

(#) For words marked with this symbol see page 44.

2. *Abbreviations*

adv.	adverb	Is.	Isaiah
Am.	Amos	Jo.	Joel
c.	common	Josh.	Joshua
Cant.	Canticles	Ju.	Judges
cf.	compare	juss.	jussive
Chr.	Chronicles	Kgs.	Kings
conj.	conjunction	Lam.	Lamentations
cstr.	construct	Lev.	Leviticus
Da.	Daniel	m.	masculine
den.	denominative	Mic.	Micah
Deut.	Deuteronomy	Neh.	Nehemiah
dim.	diminutive	Ni.	Niphal
Ec.	Ecclesiastes	Num.	Numbers
Es.	Esther	p.	page
Ex.	Exodus	Pi.	Piel
Ez.	Ezra	plu.	plural
Ezek.	Ezekiel	Pu.	Pual
f.	feminine	prep.	preposition
Gen.	Genesis	Prov.	Proverbs
Hab.	Habakkuk	Ps.	Psalm(s)
Hi.	Hiphil	ptc.	participle
Hith.	Hithpael	s.	singular
Ho.	Hophal	Sa.	Samuel
imp.	imperative	suff.	suffix
int.	interjection	t.	times
Jer.	Jeremiah	vs.	verse

vii

בְּנִי לִדְבָרַי הַקְשִׁיבָה . . .
אַל־יַלִּיזוּ מֵעֵינֶיךָ שָׁמְרֵם בְּתוֹךְ לְבָבֶךָ:

Prov. 4 : 20–21

LIST I

Verbal Roots,
Their Nominal and Other Cognates,
Occurring Ten or More Times

An Alphabetical Listing of Addenda to LIST I

אָבֵל (2)[1]   water-course, brook (13)
[Insert as No. 117a., p. 19.]

אֱמֹר (1)†   word (49, 21 in Prov.)
[Insert as No. 2a., p. 3.]

דָּרַךְ   to tread, bend the bow (62)
דֶּרֶךְ   a. way, road, journey; custom
         (over 500)
[Insert between Nos. 17c. and 18, p. 10.]

הָמַם (Qal)   to discomfit, disturb (14)
[Insert between Nos. 169a. and 170, p. 20.]

זָנַח (2)†   to reject (21)
[Insert between Nos. 86 and 87, p. 18.]

חַיִּים   life, lifetime (100-199)
[Insert as No. 10b., p. 4.]

חָפַז   to hurry away (in alarm, fright)
         (10)
[Insert between Nos. 222 and 223, p. 21.]

יָהּ   Yah (shortened form of יהוה)
       (25, 19 in Ps.)
[Insert as No. 5b., p. 3.]

יָקַץ[2] (Qal)   to awake (10)
[Insert between Nos. 223 and 224, p. 21.]

לוּן   to murmur against (Ni., Hi.) (19)
[Insert between Nos. 109 and 110, p. 19.]

לֵוִי   Levi (200-500)
[Insert as No. 174a., p. 20.]

לָכֵן   therefore (100-199)
[Add to No. 16a., p. 4.]

¹ For אָבֵל (1), see p. 13, no. 84a.

² Cf. with I G. 82, p. 18.

מִקְנָה   purchase (15)
[Insert as No. 31b., p. 9]

מַשְׂכִּיל   Hi. ptc. used as title for a type of
           poetic composition in Ps. (14)
[Insert as No. 36b., p. 9.]

נָדַד   to be aimless; homeless; shake
        (the head (25)
[Insert between Nos. 162 and 163, p. 15.]

סוּךְ   to anoint with oil (10)
[Insert between Nos. 226 and 227, p. 21.]

עַל־כֵּן   therefore
[Add to No. 17a., p. 3.]

צֶמַח   growth, a sprout (10)
[Insert as No. 119a., p. 14.]

קָדֵשׁ, קְדֵשָׁה (1)†   sacred person, temple prostitute
                    (10)
[Insert as No. 45d., p. 7.]

קַל, קַלָּה   light, swift, fleet (13)
[Insert as No. 30b., p. 9.]

רַגְלִי   one who walks on foot (12)
[Insert as No. 6b., p. 11.]

רָוָה   to drink one's fill (15)
[Insert between Nos. 163 and 164, p. 20.]

שׁוּר (1)† (Qal)   to behold, regard (16)
[Insert between Nos. 149 and 150, p. 19.]

שָׁחַח   to bow down (17)
[Insert between Nos. 138a. and 139, p. 19.]

שָׁעָה   to gaze, look at (14)
[Insert between Nos. 182 and 183, p. 20.]

תְּשׁוּעָה   deliverance, salvation (34)
[Insert as No. 15c., p. 4.]

I A. Verbs Occurring Over 500 Times

אָכַל	**1**	to eat, devour; to feed (Hi.)
אֹכֶל	a.	food (45)
מַאֲכָל	b.	food (30)
אָכְלָה	c.	food (18, 10 in Ezek.)
אָמַר	**2**	to say
אִמְרָה	a.	saying (35, 18 in Ps. 119)
בּוֹא	**3**	to go in, enter, come; to bring in (Hi.)
תְּבוּאָה	a.	increase (41)
מָבוֹא	b.	entrance (25)
דבר (2)¹	**4**	to speak (Pi.)
דָּבָר	a.	word, thing (over 500)
דְּבִיר (#)	b.	back room of temple (16, 11 in I Kgs.)
הָיָה	**5**	to be, happen
יהוה	a.	Yahweh (over 500)
הָלַךְ	**6**	to go, walk
יָדַע	**7**	to know
דַּעַת	a.	knowledge (70-99, 40 in Prov.)
מַדּוּעַ	b.	wherefore? why? (70-99)
יִדְּעֹנִי	c.	familiar spirit, sooth-sayer (11)
יָלַד	**8**	to bring forth, bear
יֶלֶד	a.	male child, boy (70-99)
יַלְדָּה (f.)		girl
תּוֹלֵדוֹת*	b.	generations (39)
מוֹלֶדֶת	c.	kindred (21)
יָלִיד*	d.	son, slave born in the household (13)
יָצָא	**9**	to go forth, out
צֹאן	a.	flock (200-299)
מוֹצָא	b.	issue, exit, utterance (27)
תּוֹצָאוֹת	c.	sources, extremities, outlets (23, 14 in Josh.)
צֶאֱצָאִים	d.	offspring (11)
יָשַׁב	**10**	to sit, dwell, inhabit
מוֹשָׁב	a.	seat, dwelling (44)
תּוֹשָׁב	b.	sojourner (14)

לָקַח	**11**	to take
לֶקַח	a.	teaching, understanding (9, 6 in Prov.)
מוּת	**12**	to die
מָוֶת	a.	death (100-199)
נָכָה	**13**	to smite (Hi.)
מַכָּה	a.	smiting, blow (45)
נָשָׂא	**14**	to lift up, bear, carry
נָשִׂיא	a.	prince (100-199)
מַשָּׂא (1, 2)	b.	burden, tribute; oracle (67)
מַשְׂאֵת	c.	a lifting up, gift (16)
שְׂאֵת	d.	dignity (14)
נָתַן	**15**	to give
מַתָּן (f.), מַתָּנָה	a.	gift (22)
נְתִינִים*	b.	(only plu.) those given to the temple, temple-servants (17, all in the Chronicler)
עָבַר (1)¹	**16**	to pass over, transgress
עֵבֶר	a.	side, region; (prep.) beyond (70-99)
בַּעֲבוּר	b.	(prep.) on account of; (conj.) in order to (49)
עִבְרִי	c.	an Hebrew (32)
עָלָה	**17**	to go up
עַל (2)†	a.	(prep.) upon, against, over (Over 500)
עֹלָה	b.	burnt-offering (200-299)
מַעַל (2)²	c.	upwards, above (100-199)
עֶלְיוֹן	d.	the upper, highest (53)
מַעֲלָה	e.	ascent, step, stair (46, in first vs. of Ps. 120-134)
עֲלִיָּה	f.	upper room (20)
מַעֲלֶה	g.	ascent, rise; stand, platform (19)
עָלֶה	h.	leaf, leafage (17)
תְּעָלָה (?) (1)†	i.	water-course, conduit (9)
עָמַד	**18**	to stand
עַמּוּד	a.	pillar, column (100-199)

¹ For דבר (1), see p. 26, no. 21

¹ For עָבַר (2), see p. 28, no. 77
² For מַעַל (1), see p. 14, no. 106a

3

*עָמַד	b.	(prep., only with suff.) with (45)	רָאָה	23	to see; to appear (Ni.); to show (Hi.)
עָשָׂה	19	to do, make	מַרְאֶה	a.	sight (100-199)
מַעֲשֶׂה	a.	work (200-299)	רֹאֶה	b.	seer (12)
צָוָה	20	to command (Pi.)	מַרְאָה	c.	vision, mirror (12)
מִצְוָה	a.	commandment (100-199)	שִׂים (Qal)	24	to set, place
קוּם	21	to rise, stand	שׁוּב	25	to turn, return
מָקוֹם	a.	place (300-500)	מְשׁוּבָה	a.	backsliding, apostasy (12, 9 in Jer.)
קוֹמָה	b.	height (46)	שָׁלַח	26	to stretch out, let go, send
קָמָה	c.	standing grain (10)	שָׁמַע	27	to hear, obey
קרא (1) [1]	22	to call, meet	שְׁמוּעָה	a.	report (27)
מִקְרָא	a.	convocation (25, 12 in Lev.)	שֵׁמַע	b.	report (17)

[1] For קרא (2), see p. 12, no. 19

I B. Verbs Occurring 200-500 Times

אהב	1	to love, like	חיה	10	to live
אַהֲבָה	a.	love (40)	חַיָּה (f.); חַי	a.	living, life (300-500); beast, wild animal (100-199)
(אֹיֵב) איב	2	to be hostile towards (all but once in Qal ptc.: enemy)	יסף	11	to add
אסף	3	to gather	יוֹסֵף	a.	Joseph (200-299)
בנה	4	to build	ירא	12	to fear
בֵּן	a.	son (over 500)	יָרֵא	a.	afraid of, fearful (61)
בַּת (1) [1]	b.	daughter (over 500)	יִרְאָה	b.	fear, reverence, awe (45)
תַּבְנִית	c.	likeness, pattern (20)	מוֹרָא	c.	terror (12)
בקש	5	to seek (Pi.)	ירד	13	to go down
ברך (2) [2]	6	to bless	ירשׁ	14	to subdue, possess, dispossess
בְּרָכָה	a.	blessing (68)	תִּירוֹשׁ	a.	new wine (38)
זכר	7	to remember	רֶשֶׁת	b.	net (22)
זִכָּרוֹן	a.	memorial (24)	יְרֻשָּׁה	c.	possession (14)
זֵכֶר	b.	remembrance (23)	ישע	15	to save, deliver (Hi., Ni.)
חזק	8	to be strong; to seize, grasp (Hi.)	יְשׁוּעָה	a.	deliverance, salvation (70-99)
חָזָק	a.	firm, strong (56)	יֵשַׁע	b.	help, salvation (36, 20 in Ps.)
חטא	9	to miss (a mark), sin	כון	16	to be firm, established (Ni.); to set up, establish (Polel); to prepare, make ready (Hi.)
חַטָּאת	a.	sin, sin-offering, expiation (200-299)	כֵּן (1, 2)	a.	thus so; firm, upright (over 500)
חֵטְא	b.	sin (35)	מְכוֹנָה	b.	base (24, 15 in I Kgs. 7)
*חַטָּא	c.	sinner; sinful (19)	מָכוֹן	c.	foundation, place (17)
			כלה	17	to cease, come to an end, finish, complete
			כָּלָה	a.	complete destruction (22)

[1] For בַּת (2). see p. 41, no. 117

For ברך (1), see p. 29. no. 98

כרת	18	to cut off, fell, exterminate; make a covenant (with בְּרִית)
כתב	19	to write
כְּתָב	a.	writing (17, 9 in Es.)
מלא	20	to be full; to fill, fulfill (Pi.)
מָלֵא (f.), מְלֵאָה	a.	full (63)
מְלֹא	b.	fullness (38)
מִלֻּאִים	c.	consecration, setting (15)
מלך (1) †	21	to reign, be king
מֶלֶךְ	a.	king (over 500); queen (35, 25 in Es.)
מַלְכָּה		
מַמְלָכָה	b.	kingdom (100-199)
מַלְכוּת	c.	kingdom (70-99)
מְלוּכָה	d.	kingdom (24)
מוצא	22	to find
נגד	23	to make known, report, tell (Hi.)
נֶגֶד	a.	(prep.) before (100-199)
נָגִיד	b.	leader (44)
נטה	24	to turn, stretch out
מַטֶּה	a.	rod, staff, tribe (200-299)
מִטָּה	b.	bed, couch (29)
מַטָּה	c.	beneath (18)
נפל	25	to fall
נצל	26	to deliver (Ni., Hi.)

סור	27	to turn aside; to take away, remove (Hi.)
עבד	28	to serve
עֶבֶד	a.	servant (over 500)
עֲבֹדָה	b.	service (100-199)
ענה (1) ¹	29	to answer
פקד	30	to visit, number, appoint, miss, take care of, muster
פְּקֻדָּה	a.	oversight visitation, punishment (32)
*פִּקוּדִים	b.	precepts (24)
פָּקִיד	c.	overseer, officer (13)
רבה (1) †	31	to be numerous, be great; to multiply, make many (Hi.)
אַרְבֶּה (?)	a.	locust (23)
שכב	32	to lie down
מִשְׁכָּב	a.	bed, place or act of lying (46)
שמר	33	to keep watch, guard
שֹׁמְרוֹן	a.	Samaria (100-199)
מִשְׁמֶרֶת	b.	guard, obligation, service (70-99)
מִשְׁמָר	c.	guard, guardpost, group of attendants (20)
שפט	34	to judge; to enter into controversy, plead (Ni.)
מִשְׁפָּט	a.	judgment, custom (300-500)
שְׁפָטִים	b.	acts of judgment (16, 10 in Ezek.)
שתה	35	to drink
מִשְׁתֶּה	a.	banquet (45, 23 in Es.)

I C. Verbs Occurring 100-199 Times

אבד	1	to perish; to destroy (Pi.); to exterminate (Hi.)
אמן	2	to be steady, firm, trustworthy, faithful (Ni.); to believe (Hi.)
אֱמֶת	a.	trustworthiness, stability, faithfulness, truth (100-199)
אֱמוּנָה	b.	faithfulness (49)
אָמֵן	c.	(it is) sure, certain; amen (25)
בוש	3	to be ashamed
בֹּשֶׁת	a.	shame (30)
בחר	4	to choose
בָּחוּר	a.	young man (44)
*בָּחִיר	b.	chosen (13)

*מִבְחָר	c.	choice (12)
בטח	5	to trust
בֶּטַח	a.	security, trust (42)
מִבְטָח	b.	trust (15)
בין	6	to understand
*בַּיִן	a.	interval;
בֵּין		(cstr.) between (over 500)
תְּבוּנָה	b.	understanding (42)
בִּינָה	c.	understanding (37)

¹ For ענה (2), see p. 9, no. 26;
ענה (3), p. 25, no. 13;
ענה (4), p. 20, no. 190

5

בכה	7	to weep
בְּכִי	a.	weeping (30)
גאל (1) [1]	8	to redeem
גְּאֻלָּה	a.	redemption (15, 9 in Lev.)
גדל	9	to become strong, great; to bring up, let grow, nourish (Pi.)
גָּדוֹל	a.	great (over 500)
מִגְדָּל	b.	tower (51)
גֹּדֶל	c.	greatness (13)
גְּדוּלָּה	d.	greatness (12)
גור (1) [2]	10	to sojourn
גֵּר	a.	stranger (70-99, 43 in Num.-Deut.)
*מְגוּרִים	b.	dwelling-place, sojourning-place (12)
גלה	11	to reveal, uncover; depart, go into exile
גּוֹלָה	a.	captivity (42)
גָּלוּת	b.	exile(s) (15)
דרש	12	to seek, inquire
מִדְרָשׁ	a.	exposition (2, II Chr. 13:22, 24:27)
הלל (2) †	13	to praise (Pi.); to boast oneself (Hith.) (87 t. in Ps.)
תְּהִלָּה	a.	praise (56, 29 in Ps.)
הרג	14	to kill
זבח	15	to slaughter
מִזְבֵּחַ	a.	altar (300-500)
זֶבַח	b.	sacrifice (100-199)
חוה	16	to bow down (Hishtaphel)
חלל (1) [3]	17	to be defiled (Ni.); to pollute, profane (Pi.); to begin (Hi.)
תְּחִלָּה	a.	beginning (23)
חָלִילָה	b.	(int.) far be it from . . . (preventive negative exclamation) (20)
חנה (1) † (Qal)	18	to encamp
מַחֲנֶה	a.	camp (200-299)
חשב	19	to account, regard, value
מַחֲשֶׁבֶת	a.	thought (54)
טמא	20	to be unclean
טָמֵא (f), טְמֵאָה	a.	unclean (70-99, 46 in Lev.)

טֻמְאָה	b.	uncleanness (37, 18 in Lev.)
ידה (2) †	21	to thank, praise, confess (Hi., Hith.)
תּוֹדָה	a.	song of thanksgiving (32)
הוֹד	b.	splendor, majesty (24)
יטב	22	to be good
יכל (Qal)	23	to be able
יתר	24	to be left, remain (Ni., Hi.)
יֶתֶר	a.	remainder (100-199)
יֹתֶרֶת	b.	caul (of liver) (11, 9 in Lev., 2 in Ex.)
יִתְרוֹן	c.	profit; pre-eminence (10, Ec.)
כבד	25	to be heavy, honored
כָּבוֹד	a.	honor, glory (200-299)
כָּבֵד (1)	b.	heavy (40)
כָּבֵד (2)	c.	liver (14, 9 in Lev.)
כסה	26	to cover, conceal (Pi.)
מִכְסֶה	a.	covering (16)
כפר	27	to cover; expiate (Pi.)
כְּפִיר	a.	young lion (31)
כַּפֹּרֶת	b.	cover, lid (26, 19 in Ex.)
כֹּפֶר (4) †	c.	ransom, reparation (13)
לבש	28	to put on, clothe
לְבוּשׁ	a.	clothing (32)
לחם (1)	29	to fight (Ni.)
מִלְחָמָה	a.	war, battle (300-500)
לֶחֶם	b.	bread (200-299);
לחם (2)>		(den.) to feed a person (6)
לכד	30	to seize, capture
נבא (den.)	31	to prophesy (Ni., Hith.)
נָבִיא	a.	prophet (300-500)
נוח (1) †	32	to rest, settle down, make quiet; lay, deposit (Hi.)
נִיחוֹחַ	a.	sweetness, odor (43, 36 in Lev.-Num.)
מְנוּחָה	b.	rest, quietness (21)
נגע	33	to touch, reach, come to
נֶגַע	a.	stroke, plague (70-99, 60 in Lev.)
נגש	34	to draw near, approach
נוס	35	to flee
נחם	36	to be sorry, repent (Ni.); to comfort, console (Pi.)
נסע	37	to depart

[1] For גאל (2), see p. 20, no. 195
[2] For גור (3), see p. 21, no. 196
[3] For חלל (2), see p. 27, no. 41

6

מַסַּע	a.	journey or journeying, stage (12, 7 in Num.)	רוּם	49	to be high, exalted
סבב	38	to turn, surround	תְּרוּמָה	a.	heave-offering (70-99)
סָבִיב	a.	(prep.) round about, surrounding (300-500)	מָרוֹם	b.	height, high (54)
			רוּץ	50	to run
סָפַר (den. of סֵפֶר)	39	to write, count, number; to recount, report, enumerate (Pi.)	רעה (1)[1]	51	to feed, graze, tend (cattle)
			רֹעֶה		Qal ptc.: shepherd
סֵפֶר	a.	book (100-199)	מִרְעֶה	a.	pasture (13)
מִסְפָּר	b.	number (100-199)	מַרְעִית	b.	pasturing (10)
סֹפֵר	c.	scribe (54)	שָׂמַח	52	to rejoice; to gladden (Pi.)
עזב	40	to leave, abandon	שִׂמְחָה	a.	rejoicing (70-99)
פנה	41	to turn about	שָׂמֵחַ	b.	joyful (21)
*פָּנֶה	a.	face (over 500); (prep.) before	שׂנא	53	to hate
<לִפְנֵי			שׂנֵא, *מְשַׂנֵּא		(Qal & Pi. ptc.: adversary, enemy)
פֶּן (?)	b.	lest (100-199)	שִׂנְאָה	a.	hatred (17)
פְּנִימִי	c.	the inner (32, 24 in Ezek.)	שׂרף	54	to burn
פִּנָּה	d.	corner (29)	שְׂרֵפָה	a.	burning (13)
פְּנִימָה	e.	within (13)	שָׁאַל	55	to ask
פָּתַח (1)[1]	42	to open; to loosen, free (Pi.)	שָׁאוּל	a.	Saul (300-500)
פֶּתַח	a.	gate, opening, entrance (100-199)	שְׁאֵלָה	b.	request (14)
			שׁאר	56	to remain, be left over (Ni., Hi.)
קבץ	43	to assemble, gather together	שְׁאֵרִית	a.	rest, remainder (67)
קבר	44	to bury	שְׁאָר	b.	remnant (25)
קֶבֶר	a.	grave (67)	שׁבע	57	to swear (Ni., Hi.)
קְבוּרָה	b.	burial, grave (14)	שֶׁבַע	a.	seven (300-500)
קדשׁ	45	to be holy; to consecrate (Pi.)	שִׁבְעִים	b.	seventy (70-99)
קֹדֶשׁ	a.	holy (thing) (300-500)	שְׁבִיעִי	c.	seventh (70-99)
קָדוֹשׁ	b.	holy (100-199)	שְׁבוּעָה	d.	oath (31)
מִקְדָּשׁ	c.	sanctuary (70-99)	שָׁבוּעַ	e.	week (20)
קטר	46	to send an offering up in smoke (Pi.); to make smoke (Hi.)	שָׁבַר (1)[2]	58	to break; to shatter (Pi.)
קְטֹרֶת	a.	incense (70-99, 41 in Ex.-Num.)	שֶׁבֶר, שֵׁבֶר (1)[3]	a.	breaking, destruction (42)
קרב	47	to draw near	שׁחת	59	to spoil, ruin (Pi.); to be corrupt, spoiled (Ni.); to destroy (Hi.)
קֶרֶב	a.	inward part; midst (200-299)			
קָרוֹב (f.), קְרוֹבָה	b.	near (70-99)	מַשְׁחִית	a.	destroyer, destruction (36)
קָרְבָּן	c.	offering, gift (70-99, 78 in Lev.-Num.)	שׁכח	60	to forget
קָרֵב	d.	near (11)	שׁכן	61	to tent, dwell, settle
רדף	48	to pursue, persecute			

[1] For רעה (2), see p. 26, no. 36
[2] For שׁבר (2), see p. 18, no. 95
[3] For שֶׁבֶר (2), see p. 18, no. 95a

[1] For פָּתַח (2), see p. 31, no. 177

מִשְׁכָּן	a.	dwelling, tabernacle (100-199)
שָׁכֵן	b.	inhabitant (20)
שָׁלַךְ	62	to throw, cast (Hi.)
שָׁלֵם	63	to be whole, complete; to repay, recompense (Pi.); to make peace with or live in peace with (Hi.)

שָׁלוֹם	a.	peace (200-299)
שְׁלֹמֹה	b.	Solomon (100-199)
שֶׁלֶם	c.	final or peace offering (70-99, 49 in Lev.-Num.)
שָׁלֵם	d.	whole, perfect (27)
שָׁפַךְ	64	to pour out

I D. Verbs Occurring 70-99 Times

אסר	1	to bind	טוב	11	to be good, pleasant
אָסִיר , אַסִּיר	a.	prisoner (15)	טוֹב	a.	good (300-500)
אֵסָר, אִסָּר	b.	fetter, bond (11)	טוֹבָה	b.	good things, fortune (100-199)
מוֹסֵר	c.	bands (11)	טוּב	c.	good things, wealth (31)
בער (1) †	2	to consume, burn	יעץ	12	to give counsel, advise
הפך	3	to turn, overturn	עֵצָה (1) †	a.	counsel (70-99)
תַּהְפֻּכוֹת	a.	perversity, deceit (10, 9 in Prov., 1 in Deut. 32 : 20)	לין	13	to spend the night, lodge
זנה (1) †	4	to commit fornication, play the harlot	למד	14	to learn; to teach (Pi.)
תַּזְנוּת	a.	fornication (22, all in Ezek. 16 and 23)	מאס (1) †	15	to reject
זְנוּנִים	b.	fornication (11)	מכר	16	to sell
זְנוּת	c.	fornication (9)	מִמְכָּר	a.	merchandise; sale (10, 7 in Lev. 25)
זעק [1]	5	to cry out	מלט (1) †	17	to escape, save, deliver
זְעָקָה	a.	cry (18)	משח	18	to anoint
חלה	6	to be weak, sick; to soften, put in gentle mood (Pi.)	מָשִׁיחַ	a.	anointed one (39)
חֳלִי	a.	sickness (24)	מִשְׁחָה (1-2)	b.	anointing; portion (23, all but one in Ex., Lev.)
חנן (1) †	7	to be gracious, favor; to implore favor or compassion (Hith.)	משל (2) [1] (Qal)	19	to rule
חֵן	a.	grace, favor (69)	מֶמְשָׁלָה	a.	dominion (16)
חִנָּם	b.	gratis, in vain, without reason (32)	נבט	20	to look at, regard (Hi.)
תְּחִנָּה	c.	supplication (25)	נצב	21	to take one's stand, be stationed (Ni.) to set up, erect, place (Hi.)
תַּחֲנוּנִים	d.	supplication(s) (18)	מַצֵּבָה	a.	pillar (32)
חַנּוּן	e.	gracious (13)	נְצִיב	b.	garrison; pillar (12)
חפץ (1) † (Qal)	8	to please, delight	מַצָּב	c.	station, garrison (10)
חֵפֶץ	a.	delight (39)	סגר	22	to shut, close upon; to deliver up, give in one's power (Hi.)
חרה (1) †	9	to become hot, burning, angry	מִסְגֶּרֶת	a.	bulwark, rim (17)
חָרוֹן	a.	burning, anger (41)	סתר	23	to conceal, hide (Ni., Hi.)
טהר	10	to be clean (44 t. in Lev.)	סֵתֶר	a.	hiding place, secrecy (35)
טָהוֹר	a.	clean (70-99, 49 in Ex.-Lev.)			
טָהֳרָה	b.	cultic purification (13, 8 in Lev.)			

[1] Cf. with I E. 37 below

[1] For משל (1), see p. 17, no. 32

מִסְתָּר	b.	hiding place (10)		רֶכֶב	a.	chariotry (100-199)
עוּר (3) [1]	24	to arouse, awake		מֶרְכָּבָה	b.	chariot (44)
עָזַר	25	to help, assist		רָעַע (1) †	34	to be wicked, evil
עֶזְרָה	a.	help, assistance (26)		רָעָה	a.	evil (300-500)
עֵזֶר	b.	helper; succor (21)		רַע	b.	evil (200-299)
עָנָה (2) [2]	26	to be afflicted, humble; to oppress, humiliate (Pi.)		רֹעַ	c.	wickedness (19)
עָנִי	a.	afflicted, poor (70-99)		שָׂבַע	35	to satisfy, be sated with
עֳנִי	b.	poverty, affliction (36)		שָׂבֵעַ	a.	sated, satisfied (10)
עָנָו	c.	poor, humble, meek (21)		שָׂכַל	36	to have insight, comprehension; to prosper (Hi.)
עָרַךְ	27	to arrange, set in order		שֵׂכֶל, שֶׂכֶל	a.	insight, prudence (16)
עֵרֶךְ	a.	order (33, 24 in Lev.)		שָׁבַת	37	to cease, rest
מַעֲרֶכֶת	b.	row, layer (17)		שַׁבָּת	a.	sabbath (100-199)
מַעֲרָכָה	c.	battle array (12)		שַׁבָּתוֹן	b.	sabbatical observance (11, 8 in Lev.)
פָּלָא	28	to be extraordinary, wonderful (Ni., Hi.)				
פֶּלֶא	a.	wonder (13)		שָׁחַט (1) †	38	to slaughter, kill
פָּלַל (2) †	29	to pray (Hith.)		שִׁיר (שָׁר, מְשׁוֹרֵר)	39	to sing (Qal and Polel ptc.: singer)
תְּפִלָּה	a.	prayer (70-99)		שִׁיר	a.	song (70-99)
קָלַל	30	to be slight, trifling, swift; to declare cursed (Pi.); to make light, treat with contempt (Hi.)		שִׁירָה	b.	song (14)
				שִׁית (Qal)	40	to put, place
קְלָלָה	a.	curse (33)		שָׁמַד	41	to destroy, exterminate (Ni., Hi.)
קָנָה (1) †	31	to acquire, buy		שָׁמֵם	42	to be astonished; to be desolate
מִקְנֶה	a.	possession (of land, cattle) (70-99)		שְׁמָמָה	a.	desolation, waste (57)
קִנְיָן	b.	(individual) property; flock, goods (10)		שַׁמָּה	b.	astonishment, desolation (39)
				שָׁקָה	43	to give to drink (Hi.)
רָחַץ	32	to wash		שָׁרַת	44	to minister unto, serve (Pi.)
רָכַב	33	to ride				

I E. Verbs Occurring 69-50 Times

תָּקַע	1	to clap; blow (the trumpet) (68)		רְפָאִים (1,2)	b.	Rephaim (10); dead men, shades (8)
אָחַז	2	to seize, grasp (67)				
אֲחֻזָּה	a.	landed property, possession (65)		רִיב	6	to strive, contend, conduct a legal case or suit (66)
פּוּץ	3	to spread, disperse, scatter (67)		רִיב	a.	strife, case at law (62)
פָּרַשׂ	4	to spread out (67)		שָׁכַם (den.)	7	to rise early (Hi.) (66)
רָפָא	5	to heal (67)		שְׁכֶם	a.	shoulders (22)
מַרְפֵּא	a.	healing, health (13)		בָּרַח	8	to flee, run away; to chase away (Hi.) (65)
				בְּרִיחַ	a.	bar (44)
				כָּשַׁל	9	to stumble (65)
				מִכְשׁוֹל	a.	stumbling-block (14)
				מָהַר (1) †	10	to hasten (Pi.) (65)

[1] For עוּר (1), see p. 29, no. 96;
   עוּר (2), see p. 27, no. 45
[2] For עָנָה (1), see p. 5, no. 29;
   עָנָה (3), see p. 25, no. 13;
   עָנָה (4), see p. 20, no. 190

מְהֵרָה	a.	quickly (20)		פֹּעַל	a.	deed (38)
מַהֵר	b.	hastily, quickly (18)		פְּעֻלָּה	b.	wages, work (14)
נצח	11	to act as overseer, director of (Pi.); to be enduring (Ni.) (65, as Pi. ptc. in vs. 1 of 55 Ps.)		רצה (1) †	30	to be pleased, favorable (56)
נֵצַח (1) †	a.	eminence, glory; forever; as negative: never (43)		רָצוֹן	a.	pleasure, desire (56)
				חזה (Qal)	31	to see, gaze at (55)
צלח	12	to be successful, prosper (65)		חָזוֹן	a.	vision (34)
תפש	13	to catch, seize (64)		חֹזֶה	b.	seer (17)
ארר	14	to curse (63)		חִזָּיוֹן	c.	vision (9)
אוּרִים (2) † (?)	a.	Urim (8)		חתת	32	to be shattered, terrified, disheartened (55)
יצר	15	to form (63, 21 in Is. 40-55)		מְחִתָּה	a.	ruin (11)
יֵצֶר	a.	form, purpose (9)		יצק	33	to pour out (55)
קרע	16	to tear, rend (63)		אבה (Qal)	34	to be willing (54)
תמם	17	to be complete; to be consumed, exhausted, spent (63)		אֶבְיוֹן (#) (?)	a.	needy (61)
תָּמִים	a.	perfect, complete (70-99)		דבק	35	to cleave, cling (54)
תֹּם	b.	completeness (28)		כעס	36	to be discontent; to grieve, offend (Hi.) (54)
תָּם	c.	whole, complete (15)		כַּעַס	a.	vexation (21)
נצר (Qal)	18	to watch, keep guard (62)		צעק 1	37	to cry out, summon (54)
יבש	19	to become dry, wither (61)		צְעָקָה	a.	cry, lamentation (21)
יַבָּשָׁה	a.	dry land (14)		רנן	38	to jubilate, cry for joy (54)
נטע	20	to plant (60)		רִנָּה	a.	cry of joy or entreaty (33)
יכח	21	to reprove (Hi.) (59)		ברא (1) 2	39	to create (53)
תּוֹכַחַת	a.	reproof (24, 16 in Prov.)		מדד	40	to measure (53, 36 in Ezek. 40-47)
נחל	22	to inherit, take possession of (59)		מִדָּה (1) †	a.	measure (55, 26 in Ezek. 40-47)
נַחֲלָה	a.	inheritance (200-299)		מַד*	b.	cloth, garment (12)
חדל (Qal)	23	to cease (58)		ירה (3) 3 (den.)	41	to direct, instruct (Hi.) (52)
פדה	24	to redeem, ransom (58)		תּוֹרָה	a.	teaching, law (200-299)
שדד	25	to devastate, despoil (58)		נדח	42	to scatter (52)
שֹׁד (2) †	a.	violence, devastation (25)		בקע	43	to cleave, split, burst upon (51)
חלק	26	to divide, apportion (57)		בִּקְעָה	a.	valley, plain (20)
חֵלֶק	a.	lot, portion (66)		חרם (den.)	44	to destroy, devote, banish (Hi.) (51)
מַחֲלֹקֶת	b.	share (of property), division, group (41, 36 in Chr.)		חֵרֶם,חֶרֶם (1) †	a.	thing or person devoted (29)
חֶלְקָה	c.	plot of land, field (23)		כבס	45	to wash (Pi.) (51, 31 in Lev.)
רחק	27	to be remote; to remove (Hi.) (57)		פרץ	46	to break, break through (51)
רָחוֹק	a.	far, distant (70-99)		פֶּרֶץ	a.	breach (19)
מֶרְחָק	b.	far off (18)		בגד	47	to deal treacherously with (50)
זרע	28	to sow (56)				
זֶרַע	a.	seed (200-299)				
פָּעַל (Qal)	29	to do, make (56)				

1 Cf. with I D. 5 above
2 For ברא (2), see p. 30, no. 159
3 For ירה (1), see p. 14, no. 117

10

בֶּגֶד	a.	garment (200-299)	נֵכָר	b.	foreigner (36)
נכר	48	to make unrecognizable, be strange (Pi., Hith.) to inspect, acknowledge, know (Hi.) (50)	נשׂג	49	to reach, overtake (Hi.) (50)
			תעה	50	to err, go astray, stagger, become confused (50)
נָכְרִי	a.	foreign, alien (46)			

I F. Verbs Occurring 49-25 Times

מנה	1	to count; to appoint (Pi.) (29)	גִּבּוֹר	a.	mighty man, warrior (100-199)
מִן (?)	a.	(prep.) from, out of, part of; (conj.) since, than (in comparisons), on account of (over 500)	גֶּבֶר	b.	vigorous young man (65)
מָנָה	b.	portion, part (13)	גְּבוּרָה	c.	strength, strong performance (of God) (62)
עוד	2	to admonish, take as witness, bear witness (Hi.) (45)	גְּבִירָה, (גְּבֶרֶת)	d.	mistress, lady, queen-mother (17)
עוֹד	a.	yet, still, again (over 500)			
עֵד, עֵדָה (f.)	b.	witness (70-99)	גרשׁ	11	to drive out or away (47)
עֵדוּת	c.	sign of reminder, testimony (61)	מִגְרָשׁ	a.	pasture or untilled ground (100-199, 95 in Josh.-I Chr.)
שׁנה	3	to change, repeat (26)	הָמָה (Qal)	12	to make noise, be tumultuous (33)
שְׁנַיִם	a.	two (over 500)	הָמוֹן	a.	tumult, turmoil, multitude (70-99)
שָׁנָה	b.	year (over 500)	זקן	13	to be old (28)
שֵׁנִי	c.	second (100-199)	(den. of זָקֵן)		
מִשְׁנֶה	d.	second, double, copy (35)			
צדק	4	to be in the right; to do justice, pronounce or treat as just (Hi.) (41)	זָקֵן	a.	old (100-199)
			זָקָן	b.	beard (19)
צַדִּיק	a.	righteous, just (200-299)	חכם	14	to be wise (27, 13 in Prov.)
צֶדֶק	b.	righteousness (100-199)	חָכָם	a.	skilful, wise (100-199)
צְדָקָה	c.	righteousness (100-199)	חָכְמָה	b.	experience, shrewdness, wisdom (100-199)
יעד	5	to appoint, designate (29)	ישׁר	15	to be straight, right, smooth (27)
מוֹעֵד	a.	appointed place or time; season (200-299)	יָשָׁר	a.	straight, right, upright (100-199)
עֵדָה	b.	congregation (100-199)	מִישׁוֹר	b.	plain, level, uprightness (23)
רגל (den.)	6	to spy out, slander (Pi.) (26)	מֵישָׁרִים	c.	upright(ness), evenness, equity (19)
רֶגֶל	a.	foot (200-299)	יֹשֶׁר	d.	straightness, uprightness (14)
רשׁע	7	to be guilty; to live in wickedness, act guilty, condemn as guilty (Hi.) (35)	פרה	16	to be fruitful (29, 15 in Gen.)
רָשָׁע	a.	guilty, wicked (one) (200-299)	פְּרִי	a.	fruit (100-199)
רֶשַׁע, רִשְׁעָה (f.)	b.	wrong, wickedness, guilt (43)	צפה (1)[1]	17	to watch, spy, look out (37)
אור	8	to be light; to shine (Hi.) (43)	צָפוֹן	a.	north (100-199)
אוֹר	a.	light (100-199)	קהל (den.)	18	to assemble, summon (Ni., Hi.) (39)
מָאוֹר	b.	luminary (19)	קָהָל	a.	assembly, congregation (100-199)
אזן (den.)	9	to listen to, heed (Hi.) (43)			
אֹזֶן	a.	ear (100-199)			
גבר	10	to be superior over, prevail (25)			

[1] For צפה (2), see p. 13, no. 51

קְרָה [2] 6 t.)¹ (קרא)	19	to meet, befall (28)
(לִקְרַאת)		(Qal inf. > prep., over against, opposite [100-199])
קִרְיָה	a.	place, town (29)
מִקְרֶה	b.	accident, chance, fortune (10)
רחב	20	to expand; to enlarge (Hi.) (25)
רֹחַב	a.	breadth (100-199, 54 in Ezek. 40-48)
רְחוֹב	b.	open place (of town) (43)
רָחָב	c.	broad, wide, large (21)
ארך	21	to be long; to lengthen (Hi.) (34)
אֹרֶךְ	a.	length (70-99)
*אָרֵךְ	b.	long (15)
דין	22	to plead one's cause, judge (25)
דָּן	a.	Dan (70-99)
מְדִינָה	b.	district of jurisdiction, province, satrapy (43, 29 in Es.)
מָדוֹן	c.	strife (23, 19 in Prov.)
דִּין	d.	legal case, judgment (19)
חרף (2) †	23	to taunt, reproach (40)
חֶרְפָּה	a.	reproach, disgrace (70-99)
עוּף	24	to fly (27)
עוֹף	a.	flying creatures: fowl, insects (70-99)
*עַפְעַפַּיִם	b.	eyelashes (10)
פָּשַׁע	25	to rebel, revolt against (41)
פֶּשַׁע	a.	rebellion, revolt, transgression (70-99)
צרר (1)	26	to be in distress; be narrow; wrap, shut up (34)
צָרָה	a.	distress (70-99)
צַר (1)	b.	narrow; distress, dismay (38)
צרר (2) (Qal)	27	to show hostility toward (27)
צַר (2)	a.	adversary, foe (70-99)
קדם	28	to be in front, do beforehand (Pi.) (26)
קָדִים, קָדִימָה	a.	east, eastward (69)
קֶדֶם	b.	before; east (61)
*(קֵדְמָה <) קֵדְמָה	c.	eastward (26)
קַדְמוֹנִי	d.	eastern; ancient one (10)
קַדְמֹנִיּוֹת (f. plu.),		
חלם	29	to dream (26)
חֲלוֹם	a.	dream (64, 34 in Gen.)

נָסַךְ (1) †	30	to consecrate (by pouring libations); to pour out, offer (libation) (Hi.) (25)
נֶסֶךְ, נֵסֶךְ	a.	libation (64, 33 in Num.)
מַסֵּכָה (1) †	b.	molten image (26)
נדר (Qal)	31	to vow (31)
נֶדֶר	a.	vow (60)
זמר (1) †	32	to sing, praise (Pi.) (43, 39 in Ps.)
מִזְמוֹר	a.	psalm (57, in vs. 1 of 57 Ps.)
שָׁבָה	33	to take captive (47)
שְׁבִי (f.), שִׁבְיָה	a.	captive (56)
שְׁבוּת	b.	captivity (32)
קָצַר (1)¹ (Qal)	34	to reap (35)
קָצִיר	a.	harvest (54)
יסר	35	to admonish, correct, discipline (42)
מוּסָר	a.	chastening, discipline (50, 30 in Prov.)
נבל	36	to wither, fade; to treat with contumely (Pi.) (25)
נְבֵלָה	a.	corpse (49)
נֵבֶל (?) (#)	b.	harp (38)
נָבָל	c.	stupid, impious (18)
נְבָלָה	d.	senselessness, folly (13)
נגף	37	to smite, plague (49)
מַגֵּפָה	a.	plague (26)
פרר (1) †	38	to break, destroy, frustrate, invalidate (Hi.) (49)
קוה (1) †	39	to wait for, expect (49)
תִּקְוָה	a.	hope, expectation (34)
קַו (1) †	b.	measuring line (19)
סמך	40	to support, lay one's hands on (48)
פחד	41	to fear, tremble (25)
פַּחַד	a.	trembling, dread (48)
חרש (2) ²	42	to be silent (Hi.) (47)
חֵרֵשׁ	a.	deaf (9)
יצב	43	to stand firmly (Hith.) (47)
רחם	44	to have compassion, mercy (47)
רַחֲמִים	a.	mercies (39)
רֶחֶם	b.	womb (25)
רַחוּם	c.	compassionate (13)

¹ For קָצַר (2), see p. 20, no. 163
² For חרש (1), see p. 14, no. 116

¹ For קרא (1), see p. 4, no. 22

רָצַח	45	to kill (47)	קָנָא	68	to be jealous, zealous (Pi., Hi.) (34)
אָשֵׁם	46	to do wrong, be guilty (36)	קִנְאָה	a.	ardor, passion, jealousy (43)
אָשָׁם	a.	guilt, guilt-offering (46, 28 in Lev.)	בָּדַל	69	to separate, divide (Ni., Hi.) (42)
אַשְׁמָה	b.	guilt (18)	בָּזַז	70	to plunder (42)
בָּלַע (1) †	47	to swallow (46)	בַּז	a.	booty (26)
סָלַח	48	to forgive (46)	בִּזָּה	b.	spoil (10)
עָצַר	49	to detain, restrain, retain (46)	בָּלַל	71	to mix, moisten, confound (42)
פָּגַע	50	to meet, light upon, fall upon, encounter (with hostility); entreat (46)	זוּב (Qal)	72	to flow (42)
צָפָה (2) [1]	51	to overlay, plate (Pi.) (46)	זָרָה (1) †	73	to scatter, winnow (42)
קָשַׁב	52	to give attention to (Hi.) (46)	חָרַב (1) †	74	to be dried up, desolate (37)
גִּיל (Qal)	53	to rejoice, triumph over (45)	חָרְבָּה	a.	desolate place, ruin (42)
גִּיל	a.	exultant shout, rejoicing (10)	חֹרֶב	b.	dryness, desolation (17)
מָרָה	54	to be disobedient, rebellious (45)	חָרֵב	c.	dry, waste, desolate (10)
מְרִי	a.	rebellion (23, 16 in Ezek.)	נָתַץ	75	to pull down, break (42)
רָפָה	55	to sink down, drop, weaken; to abandon, forsake (Hi.) (45)	אָמֵץ	76	to be strong, prevail; to strengthen (Pi.) (41)
חָגַר (Qal)	56	to gird (44)	אָרַב	77	to lie in ambush (41)
חִיל (חוּל) (1) [2]	57	to be in labor-pain, to tremble (44)	חָמַל (Qal)	78	to have compassion on, spare (41)
חָלַץ	58	to draw off, strip; be equipped for war (44)	יָחַל	79	to wait (Pi.); to tarry (Hi.) (41)
קָשַׁר	59	to tie together, conspire (44)	מָאֵן	80	to refuse (Pi.) (41)
קֶשֶׁר	a.	conspiracy (14)	מוֹט	81	to totter, reel, stagger (41, 27 in Ps.)
רוּעַ	60	to shout (Hi.) (44)	מוֹטָה	a.	bar, yoke (12)
תְּרוּעָה	a.	shout (36)	רָגַז	82	to quake, disturb, excite (41)
בָּזָה	61	to despise (43)	נָטַשׁ	83	to leave, forsake, abandon (40)
הָרָה	62	to conceive, become pregnant (43)	אָבַל (1) [1]	84	to mourn (39)
הָרָה	a.	pregnant (15)	אֵבֶל (אָבֵל)	a.	mourning rites, funeral ceremony (24)
הָרַס	63	to tear or throw down (43)	בָּהַל	85	to be terrified, disturbed (Ni.); to terrify, dismay (Pi.) (39)
יָסַד	64	to found, establish (43)	גָּנַב	86	to steal (39)
יְסוֹד	a.	foundation (20)	גַּנָּב	a.	thief (17)
מוּסָד (f.), מוֹסָדָה*	b.	foundation (13)	חָרַד	87	to tremble; to disturb (Hi.) (39)
נוּעַ	65	to quiver, move unsteadily (43)	נָחָה (1) †	88	to lead, guide (39)
נָקָה	66	to be clean, innocent, free from guilt (Ni.); to leave unpunished, acquit (Pi.) (41)	גָּבַהּ	89	to be high, exalted (35)
			גָּבֹהַּ	a.	high (38)
נָקִיא, נָקִי	a.	exempt, free from guilt, innocent (43)	גֹּבַהּ	b.	height (17)
			חָבָא	90	to hide (Ni., Hith.) (38)
פָּשַׁט	67	to strip or put off, make a dash for or against (43)	כָּלַם	91	to be humiliated, put to shame (Ni.); to molest, insult (Hi.) (38)

[1] For צָפָה (1), see p. 11, no. 17
[2] For חִיל (2), see p. 26, no. 22

[1] For אָבַל (2), see p. 28, no. 74

כְּלִמָּה a. insult (30)

שָׁקַט **92** to be undisturbed, quiet (38)

בָּצַר (3) † **93** to be unapproachable, impossible (Ni.); to make inaccessible (Pi.) (28) (Qal pass. ptc.: fortified, inaccessible, 25)

(בָּצוּר)

מִבְצָר a. fortified city (37)

חָסָה (Qal) **94** to seek refuge (37)

מַחְסֶה a. refuge (20)

כּוּל **95** to contain, hold in (Hi.); to supply (Pilpel) (37)

לָקַט **96** to glean, gather (37)

נוּף (1) † **97** to move to and fro, swing, wield (Hi.) (37)

תְּנוּפָה a. wave-offering (30)

עָשַׁק **98** to oppress, wrong (37)

עֹשֶׁק (f.), עָשְׁקָה a. oppression (16)

כָּרַע **99** to kneel, bow down (36)

מָשַׁךְ **100** to draw, drag; to be prolonged, postponed (Ni.) (36)

נִסָּה **101** to test, try (Pi.) (36)

פָּרַח (Qal) **102** to sprout, blossom, break forth (36)

פֶּרַח a. bud, blossom (15)

קָשָׁה **103** to be hard, difficult, stubborn (Hi.) (28)

קָשֶׁה a. hard, difficult (36)

כָּנַע **104** to be subdued, humbled (Ni., Hi.) (35, 17 in Chr.)

מוּל (1) † **105** to circumcise (35)

מָעַל (Qal) **106** to be unfaithful (35)

מַעַל (1) ¹ a. unfaithfulness, disloyalty (29)

נָקַם **107** to take vengeance, avenge (35)

נְקָמָה a. vengeance (26)

נָקָם b. vengeance (17)

שָׂחַק ² **108** to play, laugh (35)

שְׂחוֹק a. laughter, derision (16)

זָרַק (1) † **109** to sprinkle (34)

מִזְרָק a. bowl (32, 15 in Num.)

יָהַב **110** to give (Qal imp. int. formation) (34)

(הָבוּ, הָבִי, הָבָה, הַב)

מָחָה (1) † **111** to wipe off, blot out (34)

צָפַן **112** to hide, treasure up (34)

צָרַף **113** to smelt, refine (34)

קָצַף **114** to be wroth, angry (34)

קֶצֶף a. wrath (29)

חָבַשׁ **115** to bind, gird (33)

חָרַשׁ (1) ¹ **116** to plow, engrave, devise (27)

חָרָשׁ (2) † a. craftsman, engraver (33)

יָרָה (1) ² **117** to cast, shoot (33)

צוּר (1) † **118** to bind, besiege (30)

מָצוֹר a. siege (33)

מְצוּרָה (f.),

צָמַח **119** to sprout, spring up, grow (33)

חָתַן (den.) **120** to be an in-law, marry (32)

(חֹתֵן) (Qal ptc. 15 t. in Ex.)

חָתָן a. son-in-law, bridegroom (20)

יָלַל **121** to howl, wail (Hi.) (32)

כָּחַד **122** to hide (Ni., Pi.); to efface (Hi.) (32)

נָשַׁק (1) ³ **123** to kiss (32)

דָּמָה (1) ⁴ **124** to be like, resemble; to liken (Pi.) (31)

דְּמוּת a. likeness, pattern (24, 14 in Ezek.)

טָמַן **125** to hide (31)

יָצַת **126** to burn, kindle (31)

נָאַף **127** to commit adultery (31)

סָכַךְ **128** to block, make unapproachable (26)

סֻכָּה a. covert of foliage (31)

מָסָךְ b. covering, screen (25, 16 in Ex.)

שָׁטַף **129** to wash off, flood, overflow (31)

בָּחַן **130** to try, prove, examine (30)

גָּזַל **131** to tear away, plunder (30)

דָּמַם **132** to be silent, motionless (30)

נָהַג (1) † **133** to lead, drive (30)

סָפַד **134** to lament, wail (30)

מִסְפֵּד a. lamentation (16)

¹ For חרשׁ (2), see p. 12, no. 42
² For ירה (3), see p. 10, no. 41
³ For נשׁק (2), see p. 31, no. 186
⁴ For דמה (2), see p. 20, no. 168

¹ For מַעַל (2), see p. 3, no. 17c
² Cf. צחק on p. 16, no. 15

רבץ	135	to lie down (30)	חתם (den.)	150	to seal (27)
עשׁ (1) †	136	to quake, shake (30)	חוֹתָם	a.	seal (14)
רַעַשׁ	a.	quaking, rustling, rattling (17)	נדד	151	to flee, wander, run away (27)
תלה	137	to hang (30)	נתק	152	to pull off; to tear apart (Pi.); to separate (Ni.) (27)
חמם	138	to be warm, hot, inflamed (29)	נֶתֶק	a.	scab (14, Lev.)
חַמָּה	a.	heat, glow; sun (6)	שׂושׂ (Qal)	153	to rejoice (27)
מנע	139	to withhold (29)	שָׂשׂוֹן	a.	joy (22)
בשׁל	140	to boil (28)	מָשׂוֹשׂ	b.	joy (17)
חבר (2) †	141	to join, associate (28, 14 in Ex.)	אוה	154	to long or wish for (Pi., Hith.) (26)
חָבֵר	a.	companion (13)	תַּאֲוָה	a.	desire (20)
חלף (1) †	142	to pass on, over, away; to renew, change (28)	יגע	155	to grow weary, toil (26)
חֲלִיפָה	a.	change, substitute, relief (11)	יְגִיעַ *	a.	toil, labor; product, acquired property (16)
חשׂך	143	to withhold, keep back (28)	פרד	156	to separate, divide (26)
לִיץ (לוץ)	144	to deride; to be spokesman, interpreter (Hi.) (28, 18 in Prov.) (Qal ptc.: prattler, scorner, 15 t.)	פֶּרֶד	a.	mule (15)
(לֵץ)			אפה	157	to bake (25)
עלם	145	to hide, conceal (28)	הגה (1) †	158	to meditate, mutter (25)
פלט	146	to escape, bring into security (Pi.) (27)	חצב	159	to hew, hew out (25)
פְּלֵיטָה	a.	escape (28)	טרף	160	to tear, rend (25)
פָּלִיט	b.	escaped one, fugitive (19)	טֶרֶף	a.	prey, food (22)
פתה (1) † (den.)	147	to be simple, susceptible to deception, deceive (28)	טְרֵיפָה	b.	thing torn (9)
פֶּתִי	a.	simple youth (19, 15 in Prov.)	ישׁן (1) †	161	to sleep (25)
שׁפל	148	to be low; to lay low, abase, humiliate (Hi.) (28)	שֵׁנָה	a.	sleep (23)
שְׁפֵלָה	a.	lowland (20)	מרד (Qal)	162	to rebel, revolt (25)
שָׁפָל	b.	low (19)	שׁלף (Qal)	163	to draw, tear out (25)
חקר	149	to search through, explore (27)	תור	164	to spy out, explore (25)
חֵקֶר	a.	searching (12)			

I G. Verbs Occurring 24-10 Times

אחר	1	to hesitate, tarry, detain, keep back (Pi.) (18)	כהן	2	to be a priest (23, 12 in Ex.)
אַחַר	a.	(prep.) behind, after (over 500)	(den. of כֹּהֵן)		
אַחֵר	b.	another (100-199)	כֹּהֵן	a.	priest (over 500)
אַחֲרִית	c.	end, last (61)	כְּהֻנָּה	b.	priesthood (14)
מָחָר	d.	tomorrow (52)	צבא	3	to wage war; to muster (Hi.) (14)
אַחֲרוֹן	e.	at the back, last (51)	צָבָא (1) †	a.	service in war, host, army (300-500)
אָחוֹר	f.	behind, west (41)			
מָחֳרָת	g.	the next day, the morrow (32),	רבב (1) †	4	to be many, manifold, much (22)

15

רַב	a.	much, many (300-500)	עָצַם (1) †	14	to be strong, mighty, numerous (17)
רֹב	b.	multitude, abundance (100-199)	עֶצֶם	a.	bone (100-199)
רְבָבָה	c.	very large multitude, myriad, ten thousand (16)	עָצוּם	b.	mighty (30)
רָבַע (2) †	5	to have four corners, be squared (12)	צָחַק¹	15	to laugh, sport, play (13)
(den. of			יִצְחָק	a.	Isaac (100-199)
אַרְבַּע)			רָעֵב	16	to be hungry (12)
אַרְבַּע	a.	four (300-500)	רָעָב	a.	hunger, famine (100-199)
אַרְבָּעִים	b.	forty (100-199)	רָעֵב	b.	hungry (21)
רְבִיעִי	c.	fourth (56)	תָּעַב	17	to abhor, act abominably (Pi.) (22)
רוּחַ	6	to perceive, smell (Hi.) (11)	תּוֹעֵבָה	a.	abomination (100-199)
רוּחַ	a.	spirit, wind (300-500)	בָּעַל (Qal)	18	to own, rule over (16)
רֵיחַ	b.	scent, odor (58, 35 in Lev.-Num.)	בַּעַל	a.	owner, husband (70-99); Baal (70-99)
אָנַף (Qal)	7	to be angry (14)	זָרַח (Qal)	19	to beam, shine forth (18)
אַף (2)¹	a.	nose, nostril, anger (200-299)	מִזְרָח	a.	sunrise, east (70-99)
חָדַשׁ	8	to renew (Pi.) (10)	אֶזְרָח	b.	native (17)
חֹדֶשׁ	a.	new moon, month (200-299)	חָשַׁךְ	20	to be or grow dark (18)
חָדָשׁ	b.	new, recent, fresh (54)	חֹשֶׁךְ	a.	darkness (70-99)
עָוָה	9	to do wrong; to be bewildered, disconcerted (Ni.) to pervert (Hi.) (17)	עָזַז	21	to be strong, prevail; to show or appear with a defiant, bold face (Hi.) (11)
עָוֹן	a.	transgression, iniquity (200-299)	עֹז (1)²	a.	strength, power, might (70-99)
בָּלָה	10	to be worn out; to consume away, use to the full (Pi.) (16)	עֵז	b.	goat (70-99)
בִּלְתִּי	a.	not, beside (100-199)	מָעוֹז	c.	strength (35)
בַּל	b.	negation, non-existence, not (66, 31 in Ps.)	עַז	d.	strong (23)
בְּלִי	c.	without (55)	עָנַן	22	to cause to appear; to practice soothsaying (Pi.) (11)
בְּלִיַּעַל	d.	wicked, wickedness (27)	עָנָן	a.	clouds (70-99)
*בִּלְעֲדֵי,			שָׁלַל (2) †	23	to spoil, plunder (16)
בִּלְעֲדֵי	e.	apart from, besides (17)	שָׁלָל	a.	plunder, booty (70-99)
אֲבָל (#) (?)	f.	verily, alas! (11)	שָׁקַל	24	to weigh (22)
חָצָה	11	to divide (15)	שֶׁקֶל	a.	shekel (70-99)
חֲצִי	a.	half (100-199)	מִשְׁקָל	b.	weight (49)
מַחֲצִית	b.	half (16)	חָגַג (Qal)	25	to keep a pilgrim feast, to celebrate a day or feast (16)
חָקַק	12	to engrave, inscribe; enact, decree (19)	חַג	a.	feast, procession (60)
חֹק	a.	prescription, rule (100-199)	עָמַל	26	to labor, toil (20)
חֻקָּה	b.	statute, prescription (100-199)	עָמָל	a.	labor, trouble, misfortune (55)
מָעַט	13	to become few; to diminish (Hi.) (22)	עָרָה	27	to uncover, pour out (Pi.) (14)
מְעַט	a.	fewness; a little (100-199)	עֶרְוָה	a.	nakedness; pudenda (54, 31 in Lev.)
			עָרוֹם	b.	naked (16)

¹ Cf. with שָׂחַק, p. 14, no. 108

² For עַז (2), see p. 30, 147a

¹ For אַף (1), see p. 36, III D. no. 5

16

תַּעַר	c.	knife, razor (13)
עֵירֹם	d.	nakedness (10)
טבע	28	to sink down (10)
טַבַּעַת	a.	signet-ring (49, 40 in Ex.)
† פאר (2)	29	to glorify (Pi., Hith.) (13)
תִּפְאֶרֶת	a.	glory, beauty, ornament (49)
גלל	30	to roll (18)
גִּלּוּלִים	a.	idols (48, 39 in Ezek.)
גַּל	b.	heap of stones; wave (of sea) (34)
מְגִלָּה	c.	roll of book, scroll (21)
גֻּלָּה	d.	bowl, basin (14)
גֻּלְגֹּלֶת	e.	skull (12)
גַּלְגַּל	f.	wheel (11)
בְּגְלַל	g.	(prep.) on account of, for the sake of (10)
עלל (1) [1]	31	to deal with ruthlessly; to glean (20)
*מַעֲלָל	a.	deeds, practices (42)
עֲלִילָה	b.	deed (24)
משל (1) [2]	32	to say a proverb; to be like (Ni.) (17)
מָשָׁל	a.	proverbial saying (39)
רמה (2) [3]	33	to deceive, beguile (Pi.) (12)
מִרְמָה	a.	deceit, treachery (39)
† רְמִיָּה (1)	b.	slackness, looseness; deceit (15)
מטר	34	to rain (Hi.) (17)
מָטָר	a.	rain (38)
מרר	35	to be bitter (15)
מַר	a.	bitter (37)
מֹר	b.	myrrh (12, 8 in Cant.)
עשׁר	36	to be rich (17)
עֹשֶׁר	a.	wealth (37)
עָשִׁיר	b.	rich, wealthy (23)
יקר	37	to be valued, precious (11)
יָקָר	a.	rare, precious (36)
יְקָרָה (f.),		
יְקָר	b.	precious things; splendor, honor (17)
צרע	38	to be stricken with a skin disease (20)

צָרַעַת	a.	skin disease (35, 29 in Lev. 13-14)
אתה	39	to come (21)
אָתוֹן (?)	a.	female ass (34)
טבח (Qal)	40	to slaughter (11)
טַבָּח	a.	butcher, body-guard (33, 17 in Jer.)
טֶבַח	b.	slaughtering, slaughtered meat (16)
טִבְחָה (f.),		
כזב	41	to lie, deceive (16)
כָּזָב	a.	lie (31)
צוד	42	to hunt, lie in wait for (16)
מְצָד	a.	place difficult to approach, fortress (29)
מְצוּדָה(2)(f.),		
צַיִד	b.	hunting, game (19, 12 in Gen.)
צֵידָה	c.	provisions (10)
מָצוֹד	d.	hunting net, prey (9)
מְצוּדָה(1)(f.),		
שׂכר	43	to hire (20)
שָׂכָר	a.	hire, wages (28)
שָׂכִיר	b.	hireling (18)
יקשׁ	44	to snare (10)
מוֹקֵשׁ	a.	snare, bait, lure (27)
סלל	45	to cast up, build a highway (10)
מְסִלָּה	a.	highway (27)
סֹלְלָה	b.	siege, assault-rampart (11)
נדב	46	to volunteer, offer freewill offerings (Hith.) (17)
נְדָבָה	a.	voluntary offering; free will (26)
נָדִיב	b.	willing; one who gives generously; noble one (26)
צום (Qal)	47	to fast (21)
צוֹם	a.	fast, time of fasting (25)
בשׂר	48	to announce, publish good news (Pi.) (24)
גוע (Qal)	49	to expire, perish, die (24)
חום (Qal)	50	to be sorry, pity (24)
כבה	51	to be quenched, go out; to extinguish (Pi.) (24)
נאץ	52	to despise, contemn (24)
נזה	53	to sprinkle (Hi.) (24, 15 in Lev.)
נזר	54	to abstain, withdraw from (Ni.); to keep sacredly separate (Hi.) (12)

[1] For עלל (2), see p. 28, no. 71
[2] For משל (2), see p. 8, no. 19
[3] For רמה (1), see p. 28, no. 83

נֶ֫זֶר	a.	consecration, diadem (24, 12 in Num. 6)	נפץ	77	to be scattered, dispersed; to dash to pieces (Pi.) (22, 12 in Jer.)
נָזִיר	b.	consecrated one, Nazirite (16)			
† (1) סוג	55	to backslide, prove faithless; move back a boundary mark (24)	סקל	78	to stone (22)
			(1) ערב	79	to go surety for, pledge (22)
(1)†(Qal) רדה	56	to rule, dominate (24)	* (1)² מַעֲרָב	a.	articles of exchange (9, Ezek. 27)
רוש	57	to be poor (24, 16 in Prov.)			
† (2) שחר	58	to look or seek for (Pi.) (13)	עתר	80	to entreat; to make supplication (Hi.) (22)
שַׁ֫חַר	a.	the reddish light preceding dawn, dawn (24)	(Qal) פשה	81	to spread, be divulged (symptoms of a disease) (22, Lev. 13-14)
שכל	59	to be bereaved of children; to make childless, suffer a miscarriage (Pi.) (24)	קיץ	82	to awake (Hi.) (22)
			שוע	83	to cry for help (Pi.) (22)
אֶשְׁכֹּל	a.	cluster of grapes; name of a valley near Hebron (13)	שַׁוְעָה	a.	cry for help (11)
בצע	60	to cut off, finish (16)	שזר	84	to be twisted (Ho. ptc.) (22, Ex.)
בֶּ֫צַע	a.	gain, profit (23)	שען	85	to lean on, support oneself on (Ni.) (22)
גלח	61	to shave (Pi.) (23)	מִשְׁעֶ֫נֶת	a.	staff (11)
גמל	62	to deal fully, finish; to grow; do good or evil to (23)	שקף	86	to look down upon (from above) (Ni., Hi.) (22)
גְּמוּל	a.	benefits (19)	חמד	87	to desire (21)
(1)¹ חפר	63	to dig, search out (23)	חֶמְדָּה	a.	desirable things, pleasant (16)
חפש	64	to search out (23)	* מַחְמָד	b.	desire (15)
יעל	65	to profit, benefit (Hi.) (23)	חֲמֻדוֹת	c.	precious things (9, 6 in Da.)
נגש	66	to drive, press (23)	מסס	88	to melt, become weak (Ni.) (21)
נקב	67	to bore, pierce, designate (23)	נתך	89	to pour out (21)
נְקֵבָה	a.	female (22, 12 in Lev.)	נתש	90	to root out, pull up (21)
שכר	68	to drink, be drunk (19)	ספה	91	to sweep away, be consumed, destroyed (21)
שֵׁכָר	a.	beer (23)			
שִׁכּוֹר	b.	drunken (13)	פקח	92	to open the eyes (21)
גדע	69	to cut off, hew down (22)	פרס	93	to break bread; to have divided hoofs (Hi.) (14)
גרע	70	to clip, diminish, withdraw (22)	פַּרְסָה	a.	hoof (21)
† (2) זהר	71	to be mindful, warn (Ni., Hi.) (22), 16 in Ezek.)	(Qal) שאג	94	to roar (lion) (21)
זעם	72	to curse, scold (12)	(2)³ שבר	95	to buy grain; to sell (Hi.) (21, 14 in Gen.)
זַ֫עַם	a.	curse (22)	(2)⁴ שֶׁ֫בֶר	a.	corn, grain (9, 6 in Gen.)
חוש	73	to make haste, act quickly (22)	שגה	96	to err (inadvertently), commit sin (ignorantly), swerve, go astray (21)
חסר	74	to diminish, fail, lack (22)			
חָסֵר	a.	one in want of, destitute (18, 13 in Prov.)	† (1) שוה	97	to be like; to make smooth (Pi.) (21)
מַחְסוֹר	b.	want (13, 8 in Prov.)	תמך	98	to grasp, lay hold of (21)
ינק	75	to suckle, suck (22)	יחש	99	to enroll oneself by genealogy (Hith.) (20, 15 in Chr.)
יוֹנֵק	a.	suckling (12)			
כחש	76	to deny, fail, lie (22)			

¹ For ערב (4), see p. 26, no. 34
² For מַעֲרָב (2), see p. 26, no. 34b
³ For שֹׁבֶר (1), see p. 7, no. 58
⁴ For שֶׁ֫בֶר (1), see p. 7, no. 58a

¹ For חפר (2), see p. 19, no. 129

יָנָה	100	to oppress (20)
מוש (2) †	101	to depart, be removed (20)
עָרַץ (Qal)	102	to suffer a shock, tremble (15)
עָרִיץ	a.	despot, tyrant; (the) ruthless (20)
קָסַם (Qal)	103	to practice divination (20)
קֶסֶם	a.	divination, decision (11)
שָׂגַב	104	to be high, inaccessible (20)
מִשְׂגָּב	a.	secure height, refuge (17)
שִׂיחַ	105	to be concerned with a matter, consider (20, 14 in Prov.)
שִׂיחַ (2) †	a.	business, concern, talk (14)
בָּרַר	106	to select, purify, be clean (19)
בַּר (3) †	a.	grain (14)
זָמַם (Qal)	107	to ponder, cogitate, purpose, devise (13)
מְזִמָּה	a.	purpose, device, evil thought (19)
נֶזֶם (?)	b.	ring; nose-or earring (17)
יָאַל (2) †	108	to show willingness, take it upon oneself to (Hi.) (19)
לָאָה •	109	to be weary (19)
לָחַץ (Qal)	110	to squeeze, oppress, vex (19)
לַחַץ	a.	oppression (10)
עָטָה (1) †	111	to enwrap, cover (19)
רִיק	112	to pour out, draw the sword (Hi.) (19)
רֵיקָם	a.	with empty hands; without success, property, cause (16)
רֵיק	b.	empty, vain (14)
רִיק	c.	empty, idle, worthless (12)
רָצַץ	113	to crush, oppress (19)
שָׁאַב (Qal)	114	to draw water (19)
דָּכָא	115	to crush (Pi.) (18)
חָבַל (2) ¹	116	to seize as pledge (18)
יָבַל	117	to bring (Hi.) (18)
יְבוּל	a.	produce (of soil) (13)
כָּלָא	118	to restrain, shut up (18)
כֶּלֶא	a.	prison (10)
לָעַג	119	to stutter, mock, deride (18)
נָזַל	120	to trickle, flow (18)
נָטַף	121	to drop, drip (18)
סוּת	122	to allure, incite (Hi.) (18)
סָחַר	123	to go about, trade, buy (18)
סָרַר (Qal)	124	to be stubborn, rebellious (18)
צָמֵא (Qal)	125	to be thirsty (10)
צָמָא	a.	thirst (18)
צָמֵא	b.	thirsty (9)
רָמַס (Qal)	126	to tread, trample (18)
תָּכַן	127	to estimate, adjust, mete out (18)
בָּאַשׁ	128	to stink, become odious (17)
חָפֵר (2) ¹	129	to be ashamed, abashed (17)
כָּתַת	130	to crush to pieces (17)
מוּג	131	to melt, faint; to wave to and fro, swerve (Ni.); to dissolve (Polel) (17)
נָקַף (2) †	132	to go around, surround, enclose (Hi.) (17)
נָשָׁא (1)² (Qal)	133	to give a loan, lend (17)
סָכַן	134	to be of use or service (13)
Cf. סֶגֶן* (or סָגֶן*)	a.	prefect, official, head (17)
עָלַז (Qal)	135	to rejoice, exult (17)
קָדַר	136	to be dark, dirty, in mourning attire (17)
רָמַשׂ (Qal)	137	to creep (17, 10 in Gen.)
רֶמֶשׂ	a.	small animals, creeping things (17, 10 in Gen.)
רָקַע	138	to stamp, beat out (11)
רָקִיעַ	a.	firmament (17, 9 in Gen. 1)
שָׁקַד	139	to be wakeful, watch (17)
אָמַל	140	to wither, decay, fade away (Pulal) (16)
בָּעַת	141	to terrify (Pi., Ni.) (16)
דּוּשׁ	142	to tread on, thresh (16)
חָשָׁה	143	to keep silence (16)
טָבַל	144	to dip into (16)
יָצַג	145	to set, place (Hi.) (16)
מוּר	146	to exchange, alter (Hi.) (16)
נָשָׁא (2) ³	147	to beguile, deceive (Hi.) (16)
פָּרַע	148	to loosen, neglect (16)
רָגַם (Qal)	149	to stone (16)
אָזַר (den.)	150	to put on, gird (15)

¹ For חָבַל (3), see p. 20, no. 185

¹ For חָפֵר (1), see p. 18, no. 63
² For נָשָׁא (2), see no. 147 below
³ For נָשָׁא (1), see no. 133 above

אֵזוֹר	a.	loin-cloth (14, 8 in Jer. 13)
גָּזַז	151	to shear, cut (15)
גָּעַר (Qal)	152	to rebuke (13)
גְּעָרָה	a.	rebuke (15)
גָּרָה	153	to stir up (Pi.); to excite oneself (Hith.) (15)
דָּשֵׁן	154	to grow fat; to make fat (Pi.) (12)
דֶּשֶׁן	a.	fatness (15)
כָּבַשׁ	155	to subdue (15)
נָגַן	156	to play a stringed instrument (Pi.) (15)
נְגִינָה*	a.	music of a stringed instrument; mocking song (14)
נָשַׁךְ (1)¹	157	to bite (15)
עָצֵב (2)²	158	to be grieved, downhearted (15)
פּוּחַ (1, 2)†	159	to breathe, blow against, launch forth, produce (15)
פָּצָה (Qal)	160	to open the mouth (15)
צָמַת	161	to silence (15)
קָדַד (Qal)	162	to bow or kneel down (15)
קָצַר (2)³	163	to be short (15)
שָׁרַץ (Qal)	164	to swarm, teem (14)
שֶׁרֶץ	a.	swarming creatures (15)
אָרַג (Qal)	165	to weave (14)
בּוּז (Qal)	166	to despise (14)
בּוּז (f.), בּוּזָה	a.	contempt (12)
גָּדַר (Qal)	167	to build a wall (10)
גֶּדֶר, גָּדֵר	a.	wall (of stones) (14)
גְּדֵרָה*	b.	(usually plu.) penfold of stones (9)
דָּמָה (2)⁴	168	to be silent, cease (14)
דָּקַק	169	to crush; to pulverize (Hi.) (13)
דַּק	a.	thin, scarce, fine (14)
חוּל	170	to dance round dances, turn upon (14)
מָחוֹל	a.	round dance (14)
מְחֹלָה (f.),		
חֵיל, חֵל	b.	rampart (9)
חָכָה (1)†	171	to wait for (Pi.) (14)

¹ For נָשַׁךְ (2), see p. 31, no. 174
² For עָצֵב (1), see p. 29, no. 129
³ For קָצַר (1), see p. 12, no. 34
⁴ For דָּמָה (1), see p. 14, no. 124

טוּל	172	to cast from afar, cast out (Hi.) (14)
כָּרָה	173	to hollow, dig (14)
לָוָה (1)¹	174	to join, accompany (Ni.) (14)
מָחַץ (Qal)	175	to break to pieces (14)
מָרַט	176	to polish; pluck (hair) (14)
סָתַם	177	to stop up, close (14)
עָכַר	178	to be taboo, cast out from social intercourse (14)
פָּגַשׁ	179	to meet, encounter (14)
קָבַל	180	to receive, take (Pi.) (14)
קָצַץ (1)²	181	to cut off, to pieces (14)
שָׁאַף (Qal)	182	to gasp, pant after; snap at (14)
גָּזַר (1)†	183	to cut in two, in pieces (13)
זִיד (זוד)	184	to act presumptuously; to seethe, become heated or animated (Hi.) (10)
זֵד	a.	insolent, presumptuous (13)
זָדוֹן	b.	insolence, presumptuousness (11)
חָבַל (3)³	185	to act corruptly; to ruin (Pi.) (13)
חָבַק	186	to embrace (13)
חָנֵף	187	to be polluted, apostate (11)
חָנֵף	a.	alienated from God, impious (13, 8 in Job)
טָעַם (Qal)	188	to taste (11)
טַעַם	a.	taste, discernment; decree (13)
עָטַף (2)†	189	to faint, languish (13)
עָנָה (4)⁴	190	to sing (13)
רָעַם (1)†	191	to thunder, storm (13)
שׁוּט (1)†	192	to rove about (13)
שׁוֹט (1)†	a.	whip (11)
אָנַח	193	to sigh (Ni.) (12)
אֲנָחָה	a.	sigh, groan (10)
בּוּס	194	to tread down (12)
גָּאַל (2)⁵	195	to be defiled, polluted (Ni., Pu.) (12)

¹ For לָוָה (2), see p. 21, no. 200
² For קָצַץ (2), see p. 27, no. 51
³ For חָבַל (2), see p. 19, no. 116
⁴ For עָנָה (1), see p. 5, no. 29;
   עָנָה (2), see p. 9, no. 26;
   עָנָה (3), see p. 25, no. 13
⁵ For גָּאַל (1), see p. 6, no. 8

גּוּר (3)[1]	196	to be afraid of (12)
בָּגוֹר	a.	horror (10)
מְגוֹרָה (f.),		
חפה	197	to cover (12)
חרץ (1) †	198	to decide, fix, determine (12)
טוח	199	to plaster, coat (12)
לוה (2)[2]	200	to borrow, lend (12)
נפח	201	to blow upon, breathe heavily, set aflame (12)
סעד (Qal)	202	to support, uphold, sustain (12)
עות	203	to make crooked, pervert (Pi.) (12)
שרק (Qal)	204	to whistle (12)
ארשׂ	205	to become engaged, betrothed (Pi.) (11)
דקר	206	to pierce through (11)
הדף (Qal)	207	to push, thrust (11)
חשׂף (1) †	208	to strip, lay bare (11)
חשׁק	209	to be attached to, love (11)
כנס	210	to gather (11)
להט	211	to devour, scorch, burn (11)
נבע	212	to bubble, flow (Hi.) (11)

נחשׁ	213	to divine, look for omen (Pi.) (11)
נער (2)[1]	214	to shake (11)
צוק	215	to bring into straits, oppress, distress (Hi.) (11)
שׁבח (1) †	216	to praise, laud (Pi.); to boast (Hith.) (11)
שׁסה	217	to spoil, plunder (11)
שׁתל (Qal)	218	to transplant (11)
אוץ (Qal)	219	to urge, be in haste (10)
געל	220	to abhor, loathe (10)
געשׁ	221	to shake (10)
דחה	222	to push, cast or thrust down (10)
חרר (1) †	223	to be aglow; to be scorched (Ni.) (10)
נגח	224	to gore, push; to thrust at (Pi.) (10)
נגר	225	to run, flow, pour (Ni., Hi.) (10)
נהל	226	to lead (Pi.) (10)
ענג	227	to be of dainty habit, to take delight in (Hith.) (10)
פזר	228	to scatter, spread (10)
פרק	229	to tear off, rend (10)

[1] For גּוּר (1), see p. 6, no. 10
[2] For לוה (1), see p. 20, no. 174

[1] For נער (1), see p. 26, no. 23

LIST II

Verbal Roots
which Occur Less Than Ten Times,
With Their Nominal and Other Cognates
which Occur Ten or More Times

An Alphabetical Listing of Addenda to LIST II

אָהֵל (2)† (den.)   to pitch a tent

אֹהֶל (1)†   a. tent

[Insert between Nos. 8d. and 9, p. 25.]

אָנָה (3)†   to cause to occur, befall

אֵת (2)† (?)   a. (prep.) with, beside (over 500)

[Insert between Nos. 1c. and 2, p. 25.]

זוּר (2)†   to turn aside from, be estranged

זָר   a. strange, different, illicit (70-99)

[Insert between Nos. 40a. and 41, p. 27.]

חָלַק (1)[1]   to be smooth, slippery

חָלָק   a. smooth (10)

[Insert between Nos. 183a. and 184, p. 31.]

חִצְצֵר (den.)   to sound the trumpet

חֲצֹצְרָה   a. trumpet, clarion (29, 16 in Chr.)

[Insert between Nos. 89b. and 90, p. 28.]

חָרַב (2)[2] (den.)   to smite down, slaughter

חֶרֶב   a. sword (300-500)

[Insert between Nos. 11c. and 12, p. 25.]

טִפֵּף (den.) (Qal)   to trip along (Is. 3:16)

טַף   a. little children (42)

[Insert between Nos. 69a. and 70, p. 28.]

כָּנַף (den.)   to hide oneself (Ni.) (Is. 30:20)

כָּנָף   a. wing, skirt (of garment) (100-199)

[Insert between Nos. 30a. and 31, p. 26]

סִפֵּף (den.)   to stand at the threshold (Hith.)
(Ps. 84:11)

סַף   a. threshold, sill (24)

[Insert between Nos. 104a. and 105, p. 29.]

עָדַר (3)†   to be missed, lacking (Ni., Pi.)

עֵדֶר (1)†   a. flock, herd (39)

[Insert between Nos. 71a. and 72, p. 28.]

(בְּנֵי) עַמּוֹן   Ammon, Ammonites (106)

[Insert as No. 8c., p. 25.]

עָפַר (1)† (den.)   to throw (earth) at (Pi.)
(II Sa. 16:13)

עָפָר   a. dry earth, dust (100-199)

[Insert between Nos. 33a. and 34, p. 26.]

פָּטַר   to escape from, set free

פֶּטֶר,* פִּטְרָה   a. first-born (12)

[Insert between Nos. 170a. and 171, p. 31.]

---

[1] For חָלַק (2), see p. 10, No. 26.
[2] For חָרַב (1), see p. 13, No. 74.

II.

אדם	**1**	to be red, ruddy
אָדָם	a.	man, mankind (over 500)
אֲדָמָה	b.	ground (200-299)
אֱדוֹם	c.	Edom (70-99)
אשׁר (1)¹	**2**	to walk straight; to lead on, reprove (Pi.)
אֲשֶׁר	a.	who, which, that (over 500)
אֲשֵׁרָה	b.	Asherah (goddess); sacred pole set up near altar (40)
*אַשֻּׁר	c.	step (9)
כלל (Qal)	**3**	to perfect (the beauty of) (Ezek. 27 : 4, 11)
כֹּל	a.	all, every (over 500)
כָּלִיל	b.	entire, whole (15)
לבב (1) †	**4**	to cause the heart to beat (Cant. 4 : 9); to make intelligent (?) (Job 11 : 12) (Pi.)
לֵבָב, לֵב	a.	heart (over 500)
נפשׁ	**5**	to take breath, refresh oneself (Ni.)
נֶפֶשׁ	a.	throat; life, self (over 500)
עדה (1) ²	**6**	to stride (Job 28 : 8); to remove (Prov. 25 : 20)
עַד (2) ³ (?)	a.	(prep.) Unto, as far as (spatial); until, while (temporal) (over 500)
עין (Qal)	**7**	to look suspiciously at (I Sa. 18 : 9, Ps. 49 : 6)
(den. of עַיִן)		
עַיִן	a.	eye, fountain (over 500)
מַעְיָן	b.	spring, fountain (23)
עמם (1) †	**8**	to ally oneself (Ps. 47 : 10); to come up to, be a match for (Ezek. 28 : 3, 31 : 8)
עַם	a.	people (over 500)
עִם	b.	(prep.) with (over 500)
*עֻמָּה	c.	close by, exactly as (32)
אלף (2) † (den. of אֶלֶף [2])	**9**	to produce in abundance, by thousands (Hi.) (Ps. 114 : 13)
אֶלֶף (2)	a.	thousand; tribe (300-500)
אַלּוּף (2) †	b.	chief, leader (63, 40 in Gen.)

אֲלָפַיִם	c.	two thousand (31)
*אֶלֶף (1)	d.	cattle (8)
אנשׁ	**10**	to be sickly, decrease (Ni.) (II Sa. 12 : 15)
אִשָּׁה	a.	woman (300-500)
אֱנוֹשׁ	b.	man, mankind (42)
חמשׁ (den. of חָמֵשׁ)		
	11	to be in battle array; to take the fifth part of (Pi.)
חָמֵשׁ, חֲמִשָּׁה	a.	five (300-500)
חֲמִשִּׁים	b.	fifty (100-199)
חֲמִישִׁי	c.	fifth (44)
כסף	**12**	to long for, be ashamed (?)
כֶּסֶף	a.	silver (300-500)
ענה (3) ¹	**13**	to be occupied, worried by
עַתָּה	a.	now (300-500)
עֵת	b.	time (300-500)
מַעַן, לְמַעַן	c.	(prep.) for the sake of, on account of; (conj.) in order that (100-199)
יַעַן	d.	(prep.) on account of; (conj.) because (70-99)
עקב	**14**	to seize at the heel, beguile
(den. of עָקֵב)		
יַעֲקֹב	a.	Jacob (300-500)
עָקֵב	b.	heel, footprints (14)
עֵקֶב (< עָקֵב)	c.	the hindmost, end; result, reward; (conj.) on account of, therefore (15)
עשׂר	**15**	to take or give a tenth of, tithe
עֶשֶׂר, עָשָׂר	a.	ten (300-500)
עֲשָׂרָה, עֲשָׂרֵה,		
עֶשְׂרִים	b.	twenty (300-500)
מַעֲשֵׂר	c.	tenth part, tithe (31)
עִשָּׂרוֹן	d.	tenth part (30)
עֲשִׂירִי	e.	tenth (28)

¹ For אשׁר (2), see p. 28, no. 68
² For עדה (2), see p. 30, no. 155
³ For עַד (1), see p. 38, no. 1

¹ For ענה (1), see p. 5, no. 29
ענה (2), see p. 9, no. 26
ענה (4), see p. 20, no. 190

עָשׂוֹר	f.	ten (16)
(זהב <) צהב	16	to gleam (Ho.) (Ez. 8 : 27)
זָהָב	a.	gold (300-500)
שׂרר	17	to rule, conduct
שַׂר	a.	official, leader (300-500)
(den. of שׁלשׁ)		
(שׁלשׁ)	18	to divide in three parts, do or be at the third day, do for the third time. (Pi.)
שָׁלֹשׁ, שְׁלֹשָׁה	a.	three (300-500)
שְׁלִישִׁי	b.	third (100-199)
שְׁלֹשִׁים	c.	thirty (66)
שִׁלְשׁוֹם	d.	day before yesterday (25)
† שָׁלִישׁ (3)	e.	third man on a chariot; carrier of shield, adjutant (17)
ברה	19	to eat bread with, administer a patient's diet
בְּרִית	a.	covenant (200-299)
גבל (den.)	20	to set a boundary
גְּבוּל	a.	boundary, territory (200-299)
דבר (1)¹	21	to turn aside, destroy, drive back
† מִדְבָּר (1)	a.	pasturage, wilderness, steppe (200-299)
† דֶּבֶר (1)	b.	plague (49)
חיל (2)²	22	to endure (Job 20 : 21; Ps. 10 : 5)
חַיִל	a.	strength, wealth, army (200-299)
נער (1)³	23	to growl (Jer. 51 : 38)
נַעַר (?)	a.	lad, youth (200-299)
נַעֲרָה	b.	young girl, maid (70-99)
נְעוּרִים	c.	early life, youth (46)
בדד (Qal)	24	to be isolated, alone
לְבַד	a.	alone (100-199)
† בַּד (1)	b.	part, portion (2 t.); linen (23 t.); stick, stave (43 t.)
בכר	25	to bear early, new fruit; to constitute as first-born (Pi.)
בְּכוֹר	a.	first-born (100-199)
בִּכּוּרִים	b.	first-fruits (17)
בְּכֹרָה	c.	right of first-born (15)
בקר	26	to attend to, bestow care on (Pi.)
בָּקָר	a.	cows, herd, cattle (100-199)

¹ For דבר (2), see p. 3, no. 4
² For חיל (1), see p. 13, no. 57
³ For נער (2), see p. 21, no. 214

בֹּקֶר	b.	morning (100-199)
דור (Qal)	27	to stack in a circle (Ezek. 24 : 5); to circulate, dwell (Ps. 84 : 11)
דּוֹר	a.	generation, lifetime, life-span (100-19
יחד	28	to be united
יַחַד	a.	together, at the same time (100-199)
יַחְדָּו	b.	together (70-99)
יָחִיד	c.	only one, alone, solitary (12)
ימן	29	to go to the right (Hi.)
(den. of יָמִין)		
יָמִין	a.	right hand or side; south (100-199)
יְמָנִי	b.	right hand, right (30)
תֵּימָן	c.	south (24)
יחם	30	to be hot to be in breeding heat, conceive (Pi.)
חֵמָה	a.	heat, rage, wrath (100-199)
כפף	31	to bend, bow down
כַּף	a.	hand, palm (100-199)
לשׁן (den.)	32	to slander (Hi.) (Prov. 30 : 10; Ps. 101 : 5)
לָשׁוֹן	a.	tongue (100-199)
† נהר (1) (den.)	33	to stream
נָהָר	a.	stream, river (100-199)
ערב (4)¹ (den.)	34	to become evening
עֶרֶב	a.	evening (100-199)
מַעֲרָב (2)²	b.	sunset, west (14)
פעם	35	to impel, move, be disturbed
פַּעַם	a.	foot, step, time (100-199)
רעה (2)³	36	to have dealings with
רֵעַ	a.	fellow, companion, friend (100-199)
*רַעְיָה	b.	(female) companion, friend (10, 9 in Cant., 1 in Ju. 11 : 37)
שׁמן	37	to grow, be fat
(den. of שֶׁמֶן)		
שֶׁמֶן	a.	oil (100-199)
שָׁמֵן	b.	fat (10)
שׁקר	38	to deceive, deal falsely with (Pi.)
שֶׁקֶר	a.	lie, falsehood, deception (100-199)

¹ For ערב (1), see p. 18, no. 79
² For מַעֲרָב (1), see p. 18, no. 79a
³ For רעה (1), see p. 7, no. 51

אצר	39	to store up
אוֹצָר	a.	supply, store-house, treasure (70-99)
הבל (den.)	40	to be vain, empty
הֶבֶל (1) †	a.	breath, vanity, idol(s) (70-99, 37 in Ec.)
חלל (2) ¹	41	to pierce
חָלָל	a.	slain (70-99, 34 in Ezek.)
חַלּוֹן	b.	window (31)
חַלָּה	c.	ring-shaped bread (13)
חמר (2) †	42	to be reddened (Job 16 : 16)
חֲמוֹר (1) †	a.	male ass (70-99)
חֹמֶר (1)	b.	reddish-clay (17)
חֹמֶר (2)	c.	homer, dry measure; load of an ass (11)
כסל (Qal)	43	to be stupid (Jer. 10 : 8)
כְּסִיל	a.	insolent (religious); stupid, dull (in practical things) (70-90, 49 in Prov., 18 in Ec.)
כֶּסֶל (1, 2)	b.	loins; imperturbability, confidence (13)
לבן (1) ²	44	to be or make white (Hi.)
לְבָנוֹן	a.	Lebanon (70-99)
לָבָן	b.	white (27, 18 in Lev. 13)
לְבֹנָה	c.	frankincense (20)
עור (2) ³	45	to be naked (Ni.) (Hab. 3 : 9)
עוֹר	a.	skin, leather (70-99, 53 in Lev.)
קצה	46	to cut off, shorten (Pi.)
קָצֶה	a.	end, border, extremity (70-99)
קָצָה (*קְצָת)	b.	end, border, edge (33, 19 in Ex.)
קרן (den.)	47	to send out rays
קֶרֶן	a.	horn (70-99)
שׁאה (1) ⁴	48	to be desolate, waste
שְׁאוֹל	a.	Sheol, underworld (69)
כרר	49	to dance, skip (II Sa. 6:14, 16)
כִּכָּר	a.	circuit; loaf; talent (68)
כַּר (1) †	b.	ram (13)
עמק	50	to make deep
עֵמֶק	a.	vale, plain (68)
עָמֹק	b.	deep (18)
קצץ (2) ¹ (den.)	51	to come to an end (Hi.) (Ps. 55 : 24, 138 : 18)
קֵץ	a.	end (66)
גנן (Qal)	52	to enclose, fence, defend
מָגֵן (1) †	a.	shield (63)
גַּן (f.), גַּנָּה	b.	garden (57)
שׂמאל (den.)	53	to go to the left (Hi.)
שְׂמֹאל	a.	left (side), north (63)
אצל	54	to set aside, take away, reduce
אֵצֶל	a.	(prep.) beside (61)
חמס	55	to treat violently
חָמָס	a.	violence, wrong, lawlessness (60)
שׂער (1) †	56	to bristle
שָׂעִיר	a.	hairy; male goat, buck (59, 27 in Num., 23 in Lev.)
שֵׂעָר	b.	hair (36)
שְׂעֹרָה	c.	barley (33)
ארח (Qal)	57	to be on the road, wander
אֹרַח	a.	road, path, way (58)
פרשׁ	58	to declare distinctly, explain
פָּרָשׁ	a.	horseman (57)
קטן	59	to be insignificant, small
קָטֹן	a.	small (54)
קָטָן	b.	small (46)
ירע (Qal)	60	to quiver (Isa. 15 : 4)
יְרִיעָה	a.	tent curtain (53, 43 in Ex.)
שׁוא	61	to treat badly (Hi.)
שָׁוְא	a.	in vain, worthless (52)
שׁוֹאָה	b.	trouble, storm (13)
שׁנן (1) †	62	to sharpen
שֵׁן	a.	tooth (52)
אפד (Qal)	63	to make the dress close fitting (Ex. 29 : 5; Lev. 8 : 7)
אֵפוֹד	a.	ephod (50, 29 in Ex.)
צלל (3) ²	64	to be shadowy, dark (Neh. 13 : 19; Ezek. 31 : 3)
צֵל	a.	shadow (49)
גאה (Qal)	65	to be high, exalted
גָּאוֹן	a.	height; pride (49)

¹ For חלל (1), see p. 6, no. 17
² For לבן (2), see p. 31, no. 166
³ For עור (1), see p. 29, no. 96
   עור (3), see p. 9, no. 24
⁴ For שׁאה (2), see p. 30, no. 136

¹ For קצץ (1), see p. 20, no. 181
² For צלל (1), see p. 30, no. 161

גַּאֲוָה	b.	haughtiness (19)
גֵּאֶה	c.	haughty (10)
פסח	66	to be lame, limp
פֶּסַח	a.	Passover (49)
פִּסֵּחַ	b.	lame (14)
דלל (Qal)	67	to be little, low
דַּל (2) †	a.	low, helpless, poor (46)
אשׁר (2) ¹ (den.)	68	to pronounce happy, call blessed (Pi.)
*אֶשֶׁר	a.	introductory word of blessing: blessed, happy (44, 26 in Ps.)
אפס (Qal)	69	to come to an end, cease
אֶפֶס	a.	end; nothing, non-existence; notwithstanding, howbeit (42)
יפה	70	to be beautiful
יָפֶה	a.	fair, beautiful (40)
*יֳפִי	b.	beauty (18)
עלל (2) ²	71	to insert, thrust in (Job 16 : 15)
עֹל	a.	yoke (40)
חדר (Qal)	72	to surround (Ezek. 21 : 19)
חֶדֶר	a.	dark room, chamber (38)
מלל (3) †	73	to say, utter (Pi.)
מִלָּה	a.	word (38, 34 in Job)
אבל (2) ³	74	to dry up
תֵּבֵל	a.	world, continent (36)
חסד (2) † (den. of חָסִיד)	75	to act as pious (one) (Hith.)(II Sa. 22 : 26; Ps. 18 : 26)
חֶסֶד (1) †	a.	loyalty, devotion, steadfast love (200-299)
חָסִיד	b.	loyal, pious one (35, 26 in Ps.)
גשׁם	76	to send rain (Jer. 14 : 22; Ezek. 22 : 24)
גֶּשֶׁם	a.	rain (34)
עבר (2) ⁴	77	to show oneself infuriated (Hith.)
עֶבְרָה	a.	anger, fury (34)
ערל (den. of עָרְלָה)	78	to leave uncircumcised (Lev. 19 : 23; Hab. 2 : 16)
עָרֵל	a.	uncircumcised; unskilled to speak (34, 15 in Ezek.)
עָרְלָה	b.	foreskin (16)

אלה (1) †	79	to swear, curse
אָלָה	a.	curse (33)
גדד	80	to gather together against; to administer incisions to oneself
גְּדוּד (2) †	a.	band, troop; raid (33)
שׁרשׁ (den.)	81	to root out, take root
שֹׁרֶשׁ	a.	root (33)
נוה (1) † (#)	82	to reach one's aim (Hab. 2 : 5)
נָוֶה (#)	a.	pasture-ground; abode (32)
רמה (1) ¹	83	to throw, shoot
אַרְמוֹן	a.	fortified dwelling-tower (32)
עוב	84	to becloud (Hi.) (Lam. 2 : 1)
עָב (2) †	a.	clouds (31)
פסל (Qal)	85	to cut, hew stones
פֶּסֶל	a.	idol (31)
*פְּסִיל	b.	(only plur.) idol (23)
הדר	86	to honor, prefer
הָדָר	a.	ornament, splendor, majesty (30)
חנט (Qal)	87	to gain the color of ripeness (Cant. 2 : 13); to embalm (Gen. 50 : 2, 26)
חִטָּה	a.	wheat (30)
נדה (1) †	88	to exclude (Is. 66 : 5); to refuse to think of (Pi.) (Am. 6 : 3)
נִדָּה	a.	excretion; abhorrent thing; impurity, menstruation (30)
עול (1) ²	89	to act wrongfully (Pi.) (Is. 26 : 10; Ps. 71 : 4)
עַוְלָה	a.	unrighteousness, wickedness (30)
עָוֶל	b.	injustice, unrighteousness (21)
ברד (1) †	90	to hail (Is. 32 : 19)
בָּרָד	a.	hail (28, 17 in Ex.)
רכשׁ (Qal)	91	to gather property (Gen.)
רְכוּשׁ	a.	property, goods (28)
שׂרד (Qal)	92	to run away (Josh. 10 : 20)
שָׂרִיד (1) †	a.	survivor (28)
שׁקץ	93	to detest as unclean (Pi.)
שִׁקּוּץ	a.	heathen detested idol, detested thing (28)
שֶׁקֶץ	b.	detestable thing (11, 9 in Lev.)
אדר	94	to be mighty, powerful, glorious
אַדִּיר	a.	mighty (26)

¹ For אשׁר (1), see p. 25, no. 2
² For עלל (1), see p. 17, no. 31
³ For אבל (1), see p. 13, no. 84
⁴ For עבר (1), see p. 3, no. 16

¹ For רמה (2), see p. 17, no. 33
² For עול (2), see p. 29, no. 117

אַדֶּרֶת	b.	splendor; state robe or coat (12)	נַעַל	a.	sandal (22)
הוֹן	95	to regard as easy (Hi.) (Deut. 1 : 41)	פָּגַר	112	to be (too) faint, tired (Pi.) (I Sa. 30 : 10, 21)
הוֹן	a.	wealth, power (26, 18 in Prov.)	פֶּגֶר	a.	corpse (22)
עוֵּר (1) [1]	96	to make blind (Pi.)	צָעַר (Qal)	113	to be insignificant
עִוֵּר	a.	blind (26)	צָעִיר	a.	little, small, young (22)
שָׂטַן (Qal)	97	to bear a grudge, cherish animosity	רָגַע	114	to come to rest, repose
שָׂטָן	a.	adversary (26, 14 in Job 1-2)	רֶגַע	a.	moment (22)
בֵּרֵךְ (1) [2] (den.)	98	to kneel, bow down	בָּרַק (Qal)	115	to light, illumine
בֶּרֶךְ	a.	knee (25)	בָּרָק (1) †	a.	lightning (21)
עָשַׁן (Qal)	99	to smoke	נָסַס	116	to falter; run zigzag; to glitter
עָשָׁן	a.	(ascending) smoke (25)	נֵס	a.	standard, signal, sign (21)
פָּחַח (den.)	100	to be entrapped, ensnared (Hi.) (Is. 42 : 22)	עוּל (2) [1]	117	to give suck
פַּח	a.	bird-trap, snare (25)	עוֹלֵל, עוֹלָל	a.	child (21)
שָׁטַר *	101	to write (occurs only in ptc. below)	שָׁחַק (Qal)	118	to rub away, pulverize
שֹׁטֵר	a.	scribe; officer (25)	שַׁחַק	a.	dust, clouds (21)
כָּתַר	102	to surround	נָגַהּ	119	to shine
כֹּתֶרֶת *	a.	capital of pillar (24, 16 in I Kgs.)	נֹגַהּ	a.	brightness (20)
נָשַׁם (Qal)	103	to pant (Is. 42 : 14)	קָלַט (Qal)	120	to be stunted, shortened (Lev. 22 : 23)
נְשָׁמָה	a.	breath (24)	מִקְלָט	a.	refuge, asylum (20)
סָעַר	104	to grow stormy	שָׁלַג (den.)	121	to snow (Hi.) (Ps. 68 : 15)
סַעַר	a.	tempest (24)	שֶׁלֶג (1) †	a.	snow (20)
סְעָרָה (f.)			חָמֵץ (1) †	122	to be leavened
דָּמַע (Qal)	105	to shed tears (Jer. 13 : 17)	חָמֵץ	a.	leaven, what is leavened (19)
דִּמְעָה	a.	tears (23)	רַעַן	123	to grow luxuriant (Job 15 : 32)
עָטַר	106	to surround; crown a person	רַעֲנָן	a.	luxuriant, full of leaves (19)
עֲטָרָה	a.	crown, wreath (23)	שִׂיב (Qal)	124	to be gray, old (I Sa. 12 : 2; Job 15 : 10)
צָהַר	107	to press out oil (?) (Hi.) (Job 24 : 11)	שֵׂיבָה	a.	gray-headed; old age (19)
יִצְהָר	a.	oil (23)	שָׁגַג (Qal)	125	to commit error, sin inadvertently
צָהֳרַיִם	b.	midday, noon (23)	שְׁגָגָה	a.	sin of error, inadvertence (19)
שׁוּחַ (den.)	108	to run down (Prov. 2 : 18)	שׁוּק	126	to prove (too) narrow, overflow
שַׁחַת	a.	pit, grave (23)	שׁוֹק	a.	thigh (19)
שָׁחַד (Qal)	109	to give a present (Ezek. 16 : 33; Job 6 : 22)	אָפַק	127	to contain, control oneself (Hith.)
שֹׁחַד	a.	present, bribe (23)	אָפִיק	a.	channel, stream-bed (18)
חָתָה (2) †	110	to rake together	הֹוָה (1) †	128	to fall (Job 37 : 6)
מַחְתָּה	a.	fire-holder (22)	הַוָּה *	a.	destruction (18)
נָעַל	111	to lock, bar	עָצַב (1) [2]	129	to intertwine, shape (Job 10 : 8); to make an image (Jer. 44 : 19)
			עָצָב *	a.	(only plu.) idol, image (18)

[1] For עוּר (2), see p. 27, no. 45;

עוּר (3), see p. 9, no. 24

[2] For בֶּרֶךְ (2), see p. 4, no. 6

[1] For עוּל (1), see p. 28, no. 89

[2] For עֶצֶב (2), see p. 20, no. 158

קוּר (Qal)	130	to dig (for water) (II Kgs. 19 : 24; Is. 37 : 25)	
מָקוֹר	a.	well (18)	
קִין	131	to chant a lament (Polel)	
קִינָה (1) †	a.	elegy, dirge (18, 10 in Ezek.)	
חפשׁ	132	to free (Lev. 19 : 20)	
חָפְשִׁי	a.	released, emancipated from slavery (17)	
עיף (2) †	133	to be faint	
עָיֵף	a.	weary, faint (17)	
קלה (2) †	134	to be lightly esteemed, treat with contempt	
קָלוֹן	a.	ignominy, dishonor (17)	
*רכל	135	to trade (occurs only in ptc. below)	
רֹכֵל	a.	trader (17, 11 in Ezek.)	
שׁאה (2) [1]	136	to roar (Ni.) (Is. 17 : 12-13)	
שָׁאוֹן (2) †	a.	roar, din (17)	
תפף (den.)	137	to beat the timbrel	
תֹּף	a.	timbrel, tambourine (17)	
זול (Qal)	138	to lavish gold (Is. 46 : 6)	
*זוּלָה	a.	except, only (16)	
כאב	139	to be in pain; mar (Hi.)	
מַכְאוֹב	a.	pain (16)	
נטר (1) †	140	to keep, guard (Cant. 1 : 6, 8 : 11)	
מַטָּרָה	a.	target; guard (16, 11 in Jer.)	
סוף	141	to come to an end	
סוּפָה	a.	storm-wind (16)	
סמם	142	to cover with paste, perfume, paint one's face, color (Hi.) (II Kgs. 9 : 30; Job 13 : 27)	
*סַם	a.	(only plu.) paste, perfume (16, 11 in Ex.)	
קלע (2) †	143	to carve (I Kgs. 6 : 29, 32 : 35)	
*קֶלַע (2) †	a.	curtain (16, 13 in Ex.)	
קשׁשׁ	144	to gather, collect	
קַשׁ	a.	stubble (16)	
רכך	145	to be soft, timid	
רַךְ	a.	tender, delicate, weak (16)	
מתח (Qal)	146	to spread out (Is. 40 : 22)	
אַמְתַּחַת	a.	sack (15, Gen.)	
עוז	147	to take refuge	
עֹז (2) [2]	a.	protection, refuge (15)	

ציץ (1) †	148	to blossom	
ציץ (f.), ציצָה	a.	blossom; front ornament (15)	
צמד	149	to put to, attach to	
צֶמֶד	a.	couple, span (15)	
תאר	150	to turn, incline; trace, outline	
תֹּאַר	a.	form (15)	
דגל (den.)	151	to lift a banner	
דֶּגֶל	a.	banner; division of a tribe (14, 13 in Num., 1 in Cant. 2 : 4)	
דשׁא	152	to grow green (Gen. 1 : 11; Jo. 2 : 22)	
דֶּשֶׁא	a.	new grass (14)	
יגה	153	to vex, grieve, be depressed	
יָגוֹן	a.	grief, vexation (14)	
מלח (2) [1] (den.)	154	to salt	
מֶלַח (2) †	a.	salt (14)	
עדה (2) [1]	155	to deck oneself with ornaments	
עֲדִי	a.	ornaments (14)	
עצל	156	to be sluggish (Ni.) (Ju. 18 : 19)	
עָצֵל	a.	sluggish, lazy (14, Prov.)	
פתת (Qal)	157	to crumble (Lev. 2 : 6)	
פַּת	a.	bit, morsel (14)	
צעד	158	to step, march	
*צַעַד	a.	marching, pace, step (14)	
ברא (2) [2]	159	to make fat (Hi.) (I Sa. 2 : 29)	
בָּרִיא	a.	fat (13)	
צחח (Qal)	160	to be white (Lam. 4 : 7)	
מֵצַח (?)	a.	forehead (13)	
צלל (1) [3]	161	to tingle	
מְצִלְתַּיִם	a.	cymbals (13, 11 in Chr.)	
צנף (Qal)	162	to wrap (Is. 22 : 18); to wind (Lev. 16 : 4)	
מִצְנֶפֶת	a.	turban (13, 9 in Ex.)	
קנן	163	to nest, make a nest (Pi.)	
קֵן	a.	nest (13)	
דבב (Qal)	164	to flow over softly (Cant. 7 : 10)	
דֹּב	a.	bear (12)	
דִּבָּה	b.	whispering, evil report (9)	

[1] For שׁאה (1), see p. 27, no. 48
[2] For עֹז (1), see p. 16, 21a

[1] For עדה (1), see p. 25, no. 6
[2] For ברא (1), see p. 10, no. 39
[3] For צלל (3), see p. 27, no. 64

הום	165	to be in a stir, throw in disorder
מְהוּמָה	a.	confusion, consternation (12)
לבן (2) [1]	166	to make brick (Gen. 11 : 3; Ex. 5 : 7, 14)
לְבֵנָה	a.	sun-baked brick, tile (12, 7 in Ex.)
נעם (Qal)	167	to be pleasant
נָעִים	a.	pleasant, delightful (12)
נשף (Qal)	168	to blow (Ex. 15 : 10); blow upon (Is. 40 : 24)
נֶשֶׁף	a.	morning (or evening) darkness (12)
נתח	169	to cut in pieces (Pi.)
נֵתַח	a.	piece of meat (12)
עקר	170	to root up, weed cut; to hamstring (Pi.)
עָקָר	a.	barren, without offspring (12)
עֲקָרָה (f.),		
קוץ (1) †	171	to feel a loathing at
קוֹץ	a.	thorn-bush (12)
רקם	172	to variegate, weave in colors (Ex.)
רִקְמָה	a.	variegated stuff (12, 8 in Ex.)
זכך	173	to be pure, clean, bright
זַךְ	a.	pure (11)
נשך (2)[2] (den.)	174	to claim interest
נֶשֶׁךְ	a.	interest (money) (11)
עקש	175	to pervert, defraud, be guilty, crooked
עִקֵּשׁ	a.	crooked, perverted (11, 7 in Prov.)
ערם (2)[3]	176	to be crafty, cunning
עָרוּם	a.	shrewd (11, 8 in Prov.)
פתח (2)[4]	177	to engrave (Pi.)
פִּתּוּחַ	a.	engraving (11)
פתל	178	to twist, prove tortuous, astute

[1] For לבן (1), see p. 27, no. 44
[2] For נשך (1), see p. 20, no. 157
[3] For ערם (1), see no. 188 below
[4] For פתח (1), see p. 7, no. 42

פָּתִיל	a.	twisted thread, cord (11)
קצע (2) †	179	to make with a corner structure
מִקְצוֹעַ	a.	corner-post (11)
קרח (1) †	180	to make bald
קָרְחָה	a.	baldness (11)
בדק (Qal)	181	to mend, repair
בֶּדֶק	a.	breach (10, 8 in II Kgs.)
בלה (>בהל)	182	to dishearten (Pi.) (Ez. 4 : 4)
בַּלָּהָה	a.	sudden terror (10)
זנב (den.)	183	to cut off, smite the tail (Pi.) (Deut. 25 : 18, Josh. 10 : 19)
זָנָב	a.	tail, end, stump (10)
כבר	184	to multiply words (Hi.) (Job 35 : 16, 36 : 31)
כַּבִּיר	a.	great, mighty (10)
מתק	185	to be sweet
מָתוֹק	a.	sweet (10)
נשק (2) [1]	186	to be equipped with (I Chr. 12 : 2; II Chr. 17 : 17)
נֶשֶׁק	a.	equipment, armory (10)
עמר (2) †	187	to deal violently with (Hith.) (Deut. 21 : 14, 24 : 7)
עֹמֶר (2) †	a.	omer (measure of grain) (10, Ex. 16, Lev. 23)
ערם (1) [2]	188	to heap up, be gathered, dammed up (Ex. 15 : 8)
עֲרֵמָה	a.	heap (10)
פלג	189	to divide (Gen. 10 : 25; I Chr. 1 : 19); to cleave (Job 38 : 25)
פֶּלֶג (1) †	a.	artificial channel, canal (10)
קרם (Qal)	190	to bend down, stoop (Is. 46 : 1-2)
קֶרֶס*	a.	(only plu.) hook (10, Ex.)
שאן	191	to be at ease, secure
שַׁאֲנָן	a.	at ease, secure (10)
שפה	192	to sweep bare (Is. 13 : 2); to be without flesh (Job 33 : 11)
שְׁפִי	a.	bare hill; piste, track (10)

[1] For נשק (1), see p. 14, no. 123
[2] For ערם (2), see no. 176 above

LIST III

Nouns and Other Words
Without Extant Verbal Cognates
in the Hebrew Bible

An Alphabetical Listing of Addenda to LIST III

אִי (1)†   coast, island (36)

[Insert between Nos. 37 and 38, p. 38.]

אַיָּלָה   doe (10)

[Insert as No. 103a., p. 41.]

אֵילָם*   porch (of temple) (16, Ezek. 40)

[Insert between Nos. 53 and 54, p. 40.]

אֵיפֹה(א), אֵפוֹ   where?; then, so (25)

[Insert between Nos. 83 and 84, p. 39.]

אַלּוֹן (1)†   large tree (10)

[Insert between Nos. 116 and 117, p. 41.]

אָנָּא(ה)   I(we) pray(beseech) you (13)

[Insert as III B. 10a., p. 35.]

אֵשׁ[1]   fire

[Insert between Nos. 1 and 2 in list III B., p. 35.]

אַתְּ, אַתֶּן   you (fem.s. and plu.) (50-69)

[Insert as No. 13a. in List III A., p. 35.]

זוּ   this, who (14)

[Insert as No. 20a., p. 35.]

[1] Cf. with III F. 2, p. 37.

יְרִיחוֹ   Jericho (57, 29 in Josh.)

[Insert as No. 78a., p. 39.]

כִּי־אִם   unless, except, but

[Insert as No. 24a., p. 35.]

כָּכָה   thus (34)

[Insert as No. 23a., p. 35.]

כְּמוֹ   as, like

[Insert between Nos. 11 and 12 in List III D. p. 36.]

לוּ, לֻא   O that, would that, if only (22)

[Insert as No. 25b., p. 35.]

מְצוֹלָה, מְצוּלָה   depth, abyss (12)

[Insert between Nos. 98 and 99, p 41.]

עַשְׁתֵּי   one (but used only with עָשֹׂר, עֶשְׂרֵה to mean "eleven, eleventh") (19)

[Insert between Nos. 32 and 33, p. 40.]

קֶרֶשׁ   board (49, 45 in Ex.)

[Insert between Nos. 1a. and 2, p. 38.]

שִׁמְשׁוֹן   Samson (38, Ju.)

[Insert as No. 30a. in List III D., p. 37.]

III A. Words Occurring Over 500 Times

אָב	1	father	אֵלֶּה (plu. c.)		these
אָדוֹן, אֲדֹנָי	2	lord, master, the Lord	יָד	21	hand
אָח	3	brother	יוֹם	22	day
אֶחָד	4	one	יוֹמָם	a.	daily (51)
אַיִן(1)[1]	5	non-existence; as quasi-verb: there is not . . .	כֹּה	23	thus, so
אִישׁ	6	man	כִּי	24	because, for, that, when, but
אֶל	7	(prep.) unto, toward	לֹא	25	no, not (often used for permanent negation)
אַל	8	no, not (often used for temporary negation; also negative of imp. and juss.)	אוּלַי	a.	perhaps (43)
			לוּלֵי, לוּלֵא	b.	if not, unless (13)
אֱלֹהִים	9	God	מֵאָה	26	hundred
אֵל	a.	God (200-299)	מָאתַיִם	a.	two hundred (70-99)
אֱלוֹהַּ	b.	God (58, 41 in Job)	מַה	27	what? how?
אִם	10	(conj.) if, when	בַּמֶּה	a.	wherewith?
אָנֹכִי, אֲנִי	11	I	כַּמֶּה	b.	how much? how many? how long?
אֶרֶץ	12	earth	לָמָּה	c.	why?
אַתָּה,אַתְּ,אַתֶּם(m., s. and plu.)	13	you	*מַי, מַיִם	28	water
בַּיִת(cstr.),בֵּית	14	house	עִיר	29	city
גַּם	15	also	קוֹל	30	voice, sound
הוּא	16	he	רֹאשׁ (1)[1]	31	head
הִיא	17	she	רִאשׁוֹן	a.	first (100-199)
הֵם, הֵמָּה (m.)	18	they	רֵאשִׁית	b.	first, beginning (51)
הַר	19	mountain	*מְרַאֲשׁוֹת	c.	place at the head (10)
זֶה (f.), זֹאת	20	this	שֵׁם	32	name
			שָׁם	33	there

[1] For אַיִן* (2), see p. 40, no. 34

[1] For רֹאשׁ (2), see p. 41, no. 100

III B. Words Occurring 300-500 Times

אֹהֶל(#)	1	tent	חֶרֶב(#)	6	sword
בְּהֵמָה(#)	2	cattle, animals	יָם	7	sea
גּוֹי(#)	3	people, nation	כְּלִי	8	vessel, utensil
דָּם	4	blood	מִי	9	who
הִנֵּה	5	behold, lo	נָא	10	particle of entreaty: pray, now; please

נְאֻם	11	utterance	שַׁעַר (1) †	17	gate	
עוֹלָם	12	remote time (past or future); forever	שׁוֹעֵר	a.	gate-keeper (37, 20 in Chr.)	
עֵץ	13	tree (also collective)	תָּוֶךְ	18	midst	
פֶּה	14	mouth	תּוֹךְ (cstr.),			
לְפִי, כְּפִי	a.	(conj.) according to	תִּיכוֹן	a.	middle (12)	
שָׂדַי, שָׂדֶה	15	open field	תַּחַת	19	(prep.) under	
שָׁמַיִם	16	heavens	תַּחְתּוֹן, תַּחְתִּי	a.	the lower, lowest (29)	

III C. Words Occurring 200-299 Times

אֶבֶן	1	stone	מַלְאָךְ¹			
אוֹ	2	(conj.) or	(לאך >*)	10	messenger	
אַיִל (1) ¹	3	ram	מִנְחָה	11	gift, offering	
אֵם	4	mother	מִשְׁפָּחָה	12	family, clan	
אַמָּה (1) †	5	forearm, cubit	שֵׁשׁ (1) ²	13	six	
אָרוֹן	6	ark	שִׁשִּׁים	a.	sixty (58)	
בָּשָׂר	7	flesh	שִׁשִּׁי	b.	sixth (27)	
(לַיִל) לַיְלָה	8	night				
מְאֹד	9	force might; adv.: very, exceedingly				

¹ For אַיִל (3), see p. 39, no. 16

¹ Cf. with III D, 19 below

² For שֵׁשׁ (3), see p. 38, no. 31

III D. Words Occurring 100-199 Times

אָז	1	then	חָצֵר	11	permanent settlement, court, enclosure	
מֵאָז	a.	formerly, since	יַיִן	12	wine	
אָחוֹת	2	sister	יֵשׁ	13	there is (quasi-verb)	
אַךְ	3	only, surely	כָּבַשׁ,			
אֲנַחְנוּ	4	we	also כֶּשֶׂב	14	young ram (both with same meaning)	
אַף (1) ¹	5	also, even, the more so				
בָּמָה	6	high place, funerary installation	כֹּחַ	15	strength, power	
בְּעַד	7	distance; (prep.) behind, through, round about, for (the benefit of)	כָּנָף (#)	16	wing	
הֵן ²	8	behold; if	כִּסֵּא	17	seat, throne	
חוֹמָה	9	wall	כֶּרֶם (#)	18	vineyard	
חוּץ	10	place outside the house, street; (prep.) outside, without	כַּרְמֶל (#)	a.	orchard (16)	
חִיצוֹן	a.	outer, external (24, 17 in Ezek.)	מְלָאכָה¹	19	work	
			(לאך >*			
			נֶגֶב	20	the dry country, south, Negeb	

¹ For אַף (2), see p. 16, no. 7a

² Cf. with III B. 5 above, p. 35

¹ Cf. with III C. 10 above

נַחַל	21	torrent valley, wadi		שָׂפָה	27	lip
נְחֹשֶׁת	22	copper, bronze		שֵׁבֶט	28	rod, staff, tribe
נְחוּשָׁה	a.	bronze (10)		שְׁמֹנֶה	29	eight
סוּס	23	horse		שְׁמֹנִים	a.	eighty (38)
עָפָר (#)	24	dust		שְׁמִינִי	b.	eighth (30)
פַּר	25	young bull		שֶׁמֶשׁ	30	sun
פָּרָה	a.	cow (26)		תָּמִיד	31	continually; regular
רַק (2) †	26	only				

III E. Words Occurring 70-99 Times

אָוֶן	1	wickedness, iniquity		זְרוֹעַ	12	arm, forearm
אוֹת	2	sign		חֵלֶב	13	fat (47 in Lev.)
אֶרֶז	3	cedar		כְּרוּב	14	cherub (32 in Ezek.)
אֲרִי (f.), אַרְיֵה	4	lion		סֶלָה	15	selah (unexplained technical term of music or recitation) (71 in Ps.)
בֶּטֶן	5	belly, womb		פֵּאָה (1) †	16	side, rim, corner (47 in Ezek.)
בַּרְזֶל	6	iron		צוּר (1) †	17	rock
בְּתוּלָה	7	virgin		קִיר	18	wall
בְּתוּלִים	a.	stage of virginity (10)		קֶשֶׁת	19	bow
גּוֹרָל	8	lot		שׁוֹפָר	20	ram's horn, trumpet
דֶּלֶת	9	door		שׁוֹר	21	bullock, steer
הֵיכָל	10	palace, temple		שֻׁלְחָן	22	table
זָכָר	11	male				

III F. Words Occurring 69-50 Times

כָּתֵף	1	shoulder; slope, side of mountain (67)		יַעַר (1) †	11	thicket, woodland, forest (59)
אִשֶּׁה	2	fire-offering (66, 42 in Lev.)		דּוֹד	12	beloved one; uncle, cousin; love (59, 36 in Cant.)
בּוֹר	3	cistern, pit (66)		חֵץ	13	arrow (58)
שִׁפְחָה	4	maidservant (63, 28 in Gen.)		תֵּשַׁע	14	nine (58)
יְאוֹר, יְאֹר	5	River Nile; stream, river (63, 26 in Ex.)		תִּשְׁעִים	a.	ninety (19)
יָרֵךְ	6	upper thigh, hip (62)		תְּשִׁיעִי	b.	ninth (17)
יַרְכָה (f.) *	a.	backside, remotest part, innermost part (28)		אֶדֶן	15	pedestal, socket (57, 51 in Ex.)
סֶלַע	7	crag, cliff, rock (62)		אַלְמָנָה	16	widow (56)
אֵיךְ	8	how? (60)		אָמָה	17	handmaid (56)
אֵיכָה	a.	how? where? (21)		גֶּפֶן	18	vine (55)
גִּבְעָה	9	hill (60)		טֶרֶם	19	(conj.) before (55)
עֲרָבָה (2) †	10	desert (60)		גָּמָל	20	camel (54, 25 in Gen.)
				דְּבַשׁ	21	honey (54)

פֹּה	22	here, hither (54)		חֶבֶל (1) †	24	cord, rope (51)
סֹלֶת	23	wheat, groats (53, 34 in Lev.-Num.)		קָנֶה	25	reed, shaft, stalk (61)

III G. Words Occurring 49-25 Times

עַד (1) ¹	1	forever (49)		אֳנִי, אֳנִיָּה	28	ship(s); fleet (38)
לָעַד	a.	forever (21)		זַיִת	29	olive tree (38)
תְּכֵלֶת	2	violet-purple dye or wool (49, 34 in Ex.)		חֵיק	30	bosom (38)
מַצָּה	3	unleavened bread (48)		שֵׁשׁ (3) ¹	31	(Egyptian) linen (38, 32 in Ex.)
שַׂק	4	loin covering of mourning; sack-cloth (48)		תּוֹלֵעָה, תּוֹלַעַת	32	maggot, worm; crimson cloth (38, 26 in Ex.)
שַׁדַּי	5	Shaddai (48, 31 in Job)		אַרְגָּמָן	33	wool dyed with red purple (37, 25 in Ex.)
הוֹי	6	(int.) ah! alas! (47, 21 in Is.)		בְּאֵר (1) †	34	water-place, well, pit (37)
חֲנִית	7	spear (47, 30 in Sa.)		מוּל, מוֹל	35	forefront; (prep.) in front of (37)
לִשְׁכָּה	8	room, hall (47, 23 in Ezek.)		פִּילֶגֶשׁ, פִּלֶגֶשׁ	36	concubine (37)
מָתְנַיִם	9	loins (47)		צֵלָע	37	side; side-chambers, wing (37, 17 in Ex.)
אַיֵּה, אֵי	10	where? (45)		כּוֹכָב	38	star (36)
חָלָב	11	milk (45)		מוֹפֵת	39	sign, token (36)
נֵר	12	lamp (44)		אֵיפָה	40	ephah (corn measure) (35)
מְנוֹרָה	a.	lampstand (39, 19 in Ex.)		לְאֹם	41	people, nation (35)
שֶׂה	13	lamb or goat kid (44)		עֵגֶל	42	young bull (35)
יָתוֹם	14	fatherless, orphan (42)		עֲגָלָה	a.	cart, chariot (25)
טַף (#)	15	little children (42)		עֶגְלָה	b.	cow (14)
לוּחַ	16	(stone) tablet (42)		מַעְגָּל (2) †	c.	track (of wagon); course (13, 7 in Prov.)
מְעָרָה	17	cave (42)		תְּהוֹם	43	primeval ocean, deep (35)
שָׁנִי (1) †	18	scarlet (42, 26 in Ex.)		דָּג (f.), דָּגָה	44	fish (34)
מָתַי	19	when? (42)		כַּלָּה	45	bride, daughter-in-law (34)
עַד־מָתַי	a.	how long?		עֹרֶף	46	neck (33)
סָרִיס	20	court official, eunuch (42)		עֵשֶׂב	47	herb, herbage (33)
הֵנָּה (1) †	21	hither (41)		אוֹפָן	48	wheel (32, 23 in Ezek.)
כִּנּוֹר	22	zither (41)		גֹּרֶן	49	threshing-floor (32)
צַוָּאר	23	neck (41)		יוֹנָה	50	dove (32)
דָּגָן	24	corn, grain (40)		כֶּלֶב	51	dog (32)
צִפּוֹר	25	bird (40)		מְאוּמָה	52	something (32)
דַּי	26	sufficiency, enough (39)		מְאוּם,	a.	blemish, defect (22)
מִדֵּי	a.	(conj.) as often as		מְאֹם,		
תְּאֵנָה	27	fig tree (39)		מְאוֹם, מוֹם		

¹ For עַד (2), see p. 25, no. 6a

¹ For שֵׁשׁ (1), see p. 36, III C. no. 13

מֵעִים*	53	bowels, belly, inward parts (32)		עַתּוּד*	71	(only plu.) male goat, ram (29)
נֹכַח	54	(prep.) in front of, over against (32)		מְעִיל	72	sleeveless coat (28)
אֶצְבַּע	55	finger (31)		פֶּחָה	73	governor (28)
גָּג	56	roof (31)		שִׁטָּה	74	acacia (tree or wood) (28, 26 in Ex.)
טַל	57	dew, light rain (31)		תֵּבָה	75	ark (28, 26 in Gen.) (2)†
כּוֹס (1) †	58	cup, goblet (31)		אֱוִיל	76	fool, stupid person (27, 19 in Prov.)
כִּלְיָה*	59	(always plu.) kidneys (31)		יוֹבֵל	77	ram's horn, ram (27, 20 in Lev.)
נָחָשׁ (1) †	60	serpent (31)		יֶרַח	78	moon (27)
צַד (1) †	61	side, flank (31)		יֶרַח	a.	month (12)
שִׂמְלָה	62	mantle (31)		מָעוֹן (1) †	79	hiding place, dwelling (27)
לַהַב (f.), לֶהָבָה	63	flame; blade (30)		סוּף (יַם סוּף)	80	rushes, reeds, waterplants (most often in expression: "Reed Sea") (27)
סִיר	64	pot (30)		טוּר	81	course, row (26)
רִמּוֹן	65	pomegranate (30)		נֶשֶׁר	82	eagle, vulture (26)
בֶּשֶׂם, בֹּשֶׂם	66	balsam-tree (29)		נָתִיב	83	path, way (26)
זִמָּה	67	loose conduct (sexually) (29, 14 in Ex.)		נְתִיבָה (f.),		
חֲצֹצְרָה (#)68		trumpet, clarion (29, 16 in Chr.)		פָּרֹכֶת	84	curtain (25, 15 in Ex.)
כֻּתֹּנֶת, כְּתֹנֶת	69	tunic, linen garment (29)		פִּתְאֹם	85	suddenly, surprisingly (25)
מִין*	70	kind, species (29, 15 in Gen.)				

III H. Words Occurring 24-10 Times

אִוֶּלֶת¹	1	foolishness (24, 22 in Prov.)		כִּיּוֹר	13	basin, pot (23)
אֵיד	2	calamity, disaster (24)		מַס	14	forced service, taskwork, corvée (23)
חֹשֶׁן	3	breastpiece of high priest (24, 23 in Ex., 1 in Lev. 8 : 8)		אוֹי	15	woe, alas (22)
יָתֵד	4	peg, tent-pin (24)		אַיִל (3) ¹	16	pillar (22, 21 in Ezek. 40-41; 1 in I Kgs. 6 : 31)
סַף (2) †(#)	5	threshold, sill (24)		אֹפֶל (אָפֵל)		
עֲבֹת	6	rope, cord (24)		אֲפֵלָה (f.),	17	darkness (22)
שַׁד*	7	(female) breast (most often in dual) (24)		אֵפֶר	18	dust (22)
אַבִּיר (אָבִיר)	8	strong, powerful; stallion (23)		דָּת	19	law, order, decree (22, 20 in Es.)
תְּמוֹל	9	yesterday (23)		לְחִי	20	jaw, cheek (21)
(אֶתְמוֹל)				מַת*	21	(only plu.) men (21)
תְּמוֹל שִׁלְשׁוֹם	a.	day before yesterday (15)		סוֹד	22	confidential talk; group of intimates, secret council (21)
גַּי, גַּיְא	10	valley (23)		סֶרֶן*	23	(only plu.) lords (of the Philistines) (21)
הִין	11	liquid measure (23, 12 in Num.)		אֱלִיל	24	gods (idols); nought, vain (20)
חוֹל (1) †	12	sand, mud (23)				

¹ Cf. with III G. no. 76 above

¹ For אַיִל (1), see p. 36, III C. 3

בְּרוֹשׁ	25	Phoenician juniper (20)	צֶמֶר	58	wool (16)
† (1) חָצִיר	26	green grass (20)	שְׂבָכָה	59	net, grating, lattice-work (16)
† (2) צִנָּה	27	shield (20)	(#)שַׂלְמָה	60	mantle, wrapper (16)
תֹּהוּ	28	waterless, impassable desert; emptiness (20, 11 in Is.)	שְׁאֵר	61	flesh, body (16)
			אֲהָהּ	62	(int.) alas! (15)
† (1) אוּלָם	29	in front of, opposite; but (19)	יֶקֶב	63	wine-press (15)
אוֹן	30	generative power, wealth (19)	מֹאזְנַיִם	64	scales, balances (15)
מְזוּזָה	31	door-post (19)	מְחִיר	65	price, hire (15)
עֵנָב	32	grapes (19)	† (1) מָן	66	manna (15)
קַיִץ	33	summer; summer fruit (19)	עֲרָפֶל	67	darkness, gloom (15)
*אַיִן (2)¹	34	whence? (18)	רֹמַח	68	lance (15)
מֵאַיִן,			† (1) שִׁבֹּלֶת	69	ear of grain (15)
אָנָה, אָנָה, אָן	a.	whither, where to (26)	תַּנּוּר	70	stove, fire-pot (15)
אָכֵן	35	surely (18)	תְּרָפִים	71	household gods, idols (15)
בִּירָה	36	citadel, castle (18, 10 in Es.)	אֵיתָן	72	everflowing stream; durable, lasting (14)
חֵךְ	37	palate, gums (18)	כַּפְתּוֹר (1)	73	knob, bulb; capital of pillar (14, 12 in Ex.)
כַּד	38	pitcher (18)	כַּפְתּוֹר (2)		Cf. Crete, 6 t.
מַקֵּל	39	rod, twig, staff (18)	לַפִּיד	74	torch (14)
צְבִי (1)²	40	decoration, beauty (18)	עֹפֶל	75	tumor, boils; knoll, hillock (14)
צַלְמָוֶת	41	darkness (18, 10 in Job)	צְבִי (2)¹	76	gazelle (14)
אוֹב	42	spirit of the dead (17)	קֶמַח	77	flour (14)
אֵימָה	43	fright, horror (17)	† (2) תּוֹר	78	turtle-dove (14, 8 in Lev.)
בְּרֵכָה	44	pool, pond (17)	תַּחַשׁ	79	porpoise; tachash-skin (14)
גְּדִי	45	kid (17)	*תַּן	80	(only plu.) jackal (14)
גֶּחָל, גַּחַל	46	charcoal, glowing charcoals (17)	תַּנִּין	81	sea-monster, serpent, dragon (14)
גַּחֶלֶת (f.),			(אַכְזָר) אַכְזָרִי	82	cruel (13)
דָּרוֹם	47	south (17, 12 in Ezek.)	אֵלָה	83	species of big tree: oak (?) (13)
חִידָה	48	riddle (17)	גַּב	84	back, rim (of wheel) (13)
חֶרֶשׂ	49	potsherd (17)	גְּוִיָּה	85	body, corpse (13)
צֶלֶם	50	image (17)	וָו	86	hook, peg (13, Ex.)
קְעָרָה	51	platter (17, 15 in Num.)	† (1) *חֹר	87	(only plu.) freedmen, noble ones (13)
† (1) שׁוֹשָׁן	52	lily, lotus (17)	חָזֶה	88	breast (13, 8 in Lev.)
תֶּבֶן	53	straw, chaff, fodder (17)	טִיט	89	clay, mud (13)
הָלְאָה	54	onwards, further (16)	יְשִׁימוֹן	90	wilderness (13)
סַל	55	basket (16)	לֻלָאֹת	91	loops, nooses (13, Ex.)
*פֵּשֶׁת	56	flax, linen (16)	מַבּוּל	92	heavenly ocean, deluge (13, 12 in Gen., 1 in Ps. 29 : 10)
צִיָּה	57	dry country, waterless region (16)			

¹ For אַיִן (1), see p. 35, III A. no. 5

² For צְבִי (2), see no. 76 below

¹ For צְבִי (1), no. 40 above

צְפַרְדֵּעַ	93	frogs (13, 11 in Ex.)
שְׁחִין	94	boil, inflamed spot (13)
תָּא	95	guard chamber (13, 11 in Ezek.)
בֹּהֶן	96	thumb, finger, toe (12)
חוֹחַ	97	thorns, spiniferous plants (12)
לָבִיא	98	lion (12)
קָצִין	99	chief, ruler (12)
רֹאשׁ (2) [1]	100	poisonous herb, venom (12)
תּוּשִׁיָּה	101	effectual working; sound wisdom (?) (12)
† תָּמָר (1)	102	date-palm (12)
תִּמֹרָה	a.	(dim.) palm-figure, ornament (18)
אַיָּל	103	stag, buck (11)
בַּהֶרֶת	104	spot, blotch on skin (11, Lev.)
גָּזִית	105	hewing; ashlar (11)
הֲלֹם	106	hither (11)
חָמוֹת	107	mother-in-law (11, 10 in Ruth, 1 in Mic. 7 : 6)
(> חָם [1] †)		(father-in-law)

סַפִּיר	108	lapis-lazuli (11)
*עָמִית	109	fellow (of people or company) (11, Lev.)
קָדְקֹד	110	vertex, head (11)
שֹׁהַם	111	carnelian (11)
*שׁוּל	112	(only plu.) skirt, lowest hem of garment (11)
† שָׁמִיר (1)	113	thornbush (11, 8 in Is.)
*אֲגַם	114	reedy pool, swamp (10)
אִגֶּרֶת	115	letter (10)
אֵזוֹב	116	hyssop (10)
בַּת (2) [1]	117	(liquid) measure (10)
גָּבִיעַ	118	cup (10)
חֲלָצַיִם	119	loins (10)
עֹרֵב	120	raven (10)
פֶּרֶא	121	onager (10)
שְׁרִרוּת	122	stubbornness (10, 8 in Jer.)

[1] For רֹאשׁ (1), see p. 35, no. 31

[1] For בַּת (1), see p. 4, no. 4b

Appendix

PROPER AND PLACE NAMES OCCURRING OVER 70 TIMES IN THE OLD TESTAMENT[1]

Arranged in Decreasing Frequency Order

יִשְׂרָאֵל	1.	Israel	אַשּׁוּר	20.	Assyria
דָּוִד	2.	David	שְׁמוּאֵל	21.	Samuel
יְהוּדָה	3.	Judah	מְנַשֶּׁה	22.	Manasseh
יְהוּדִי		Judean	גִּלְעָד	23.	Gilead
מֹשֶׁה	4.	Moses	חִזְקִיָּהוּ	24.	Hezekiah
מִצְרַיִם	5.	Egypt	יְהוֹנָתָן	25.	Jonathan
מִצְרִי		Egyptian	יָרָבְעָם	26.	Jeroboam
יְרוּשָׁלַ͏ִם	6.	Jerusalem	אַבְשָׁלוֹם	27.	Absalom
אַהֲרֹן	7.	Aaron	עֵשָׂו	28.	Esau
פְּלִשְׁתִּי	8.	Philistine	אַחְאָב	29.	Ahab
פַּרְעֹה	9.	Pharaoh	כְּנַעַן	30.	Canaan
בָּבֶל	10.	Babylon	כְּנַעֲנִי		Canaanite
יְהוֹשׁוּעַ	11.	Joshua	יְהוֹשָׁפָט	31.	Jehoshaphat
יַרְדֵּן(#)	12.	Jordan	אֱמֹרִי	32.	Amorite
מוֹאָב	13.	Moab	דָּנִיֵּאל	33.	Daniel
אֶפְרַיִם	14.	Ephraim	כַּשְׂדִּים	34.	Chaldeans
בִּנְיָמִין	15.	Benjamin	אֶלְעָזָר	35.	Eleazar
צִיּוֹן	16.	Zion	אֵלִיָּה, אֵלִיָּהוּ	36.	Elijah
אֲרָם	17.	Aram	בֵּית־אֵל	37.	Bethel
יוֹאָב	18.	Joab	גָּד	38.	Gad
יִרְמְיָה, יִרְמְיָהוּ	19.	Jeremiah	רְאוּבֵן	39.	Reuben

[1] I.e., those not derived from one simple root or stem attested ten or more times elsewhere in the Old Testament (for which see above in the lists).

Addendum: אַבְרָם, אַבְרָהָם , Abram, Abraham, should appear between Nos. 7 and 8 above.

43

Word Rearrangements

All words in the vocabulary lists marked with (#) should be rearranged as specified below.
(In alphabetical order)

P. 10, No. 34a.	אֶבְיוֹן	Move between Nos. 7 and 8, in list III F., p. 37.
P. 16, No. 10f.	אָבֵל	Move between Nos. 102a. and 103 in list III H., p. 41.
P. 35, III B.1	אֹהֶל	Move between Nos. 8d. and 9, p. 25 (see p. 24).
P. 35, III B.2	בְּהֵמָה	Move between Nos. 5 and 6 in list III D., p. 36.
P. 35, III B.3	גּוֹי	Move between Nos. 14 and 15 in list III A., p. 35.
P. 3, No. 4b.	דְּבִיר	Move to p. 26 as No. 21c.
P. 39, No. 68	חֲצֹצְרָה	Move with its den. to page 28 between Nos. 89b. and 90 (see p. 24).
P. 35, III B.6	חֶרֶב	Move with its den. to p. 25 between Nos. 11c. and 12 (see p. 24).
P. 38, No. 15	טַף	Move with its den. between Nos. 69a and 70, p. 28 (see p. 24).
P. 43, No. 12	יַרְדֵּן	Move to p. 4 as No. 13a.
P. 36, III D, 16	כָּנָף	Move with its den. between Nos. 30a and 31, p. 26 (see p. 24).
P. 36, No. 18, 18a.	כֶּרֶם, כַּרְמֶל	Move between Nos. 14 and 15 in list III E., p. 37.
P. 12, No. 36b.	נֵבֶל(2)†	Move between Nos. 30 and 31 in list III G., p. 38.
P. 28, No. 82, 82a.	נוה	Move between Nos. 68a. and 69 on p. 28.
P. 39, III H.5	סַף	Move with its den. between Nos. 104a. and 105, p. 29 (see p. 24).
P. 37, No. 24	עָפָר	Move with its den. between Nos. 33a. and 34, p. 26 (see p. 24).
P. 40, No. 60	שְׁלֹמֹה	Move to p. 39 as No. 62a.

Index

All verbal roots are unpointed. Cognates and other words are also unpointed, except in cases of homographs, where sufficient pointing is indicated to distinguish them. The first number (reading from left to right) represents the number of the page on which the word is found; the second number indicates the number of the word on that page. Where two words occasionally have the same number on the same page, their list and section are also given. Addenda on pages 2, 24, 34, and 43 are not included.

אפֶר 39,18
אפרים 43,14
אצבע 39,55
אצל 27,54
אֵצֶל 27,54a
אצר 27,39
ארב 13,77
ארבה 5,31a
ארבע 16,5a
ארבעים 16,5b
ארג 20,165
ארגמן 38,33
ארון 36, III C. 6
ארז 37, III E. 3
ארח 27,57
אֹרַח 27,57a
ארי, אריה 37, III E. 4
אֶרֶךְ 12,21
אָרֵךְ 12,21a
אָרֶךְ 12 21b
ארם 43,17
ארמון 28,83a
ארץ 35,12
ארר 10,14
ארש 21,205
אִשָּׁה 25,10a
אִשֶּׁה 37, III F. 2
אַשּׁור 43,20
אשכל 18,59a
אשם 13,46
אָשָׁם 13,46a
אשמה 13,46b
אשֶר (1) 25,2
אֲשֶׁר (2) 28,68
אֲשֶׁר 25,2a
אֲשֶׁר 28,68a
אָשֵׁר 25,2c
אֲשׁרה 25,2b
אתה 17,39
אַתָּה, אַתֶּם 35,13
אתון 17,39a

ב

באר 38,34
בְּאֵשׁ 19,128
בבל 43,10
בגד 10,47

בֶּגֶד 11,47a
בגלל 17,30g
בד 26,24b
בדד 26,24
בדל 13,69
בדק 31,181
בֶּדֶק 31,181a
בהל 13,85
בהמה 35, III B. 2
בהן 41,96
בהרת 41,104
בוא 3,3
בוז 20,166
בוז, בוזה 20,166a
בוס 20,194
בור 37, III F. 3
בוש 5,3
בז 13,70a
בזה 13,61
בִּזָּה 13,70b
בֻּז 13,70
בחור 5,4a
בחיר 5,4b
בחן 14,130
בחר 5,4
בטח 5,5
בֶּטַח 5,5a
בטן 37, III E. 5
בין 5,6
בַּיִן, בֵּין 5,6a
בינה 5,6c
בירה 40,36
בַּיִת, בֵּית 35,14
ביתאל 43,37
בכה 6,7
בכור 26,25a
בכורים 26,25b
בכי 6,7a
בכר 26,25
בכרה 26,25c
בל 16,10b
בלה 16,10
בלה 31,182
בלהה 31,182a
בלי 16,10c
בליעל 16,10d
בלל 13,71

בלע 13,47
בלעדי 16,10e
בלתי 16,10a
בְּמָה 35,27a
בָּמָה 36, III D. 6
בֵּן 4,4a
בנה 4,4
בנימין 43,15
בעבור 3,16b
בעד 36, III D. 7
בעל 16,18
בַּעַל 16,18a
בער 8,2
בעת 19,141
בצע 18,60
בֶּצַע 18,60a
בצר, בצור 14,93
בקע 10,43
בקעה 10,43a
בקר 26,26
בָּקָר 26,26a
בֹּקֶר 26,26b
בקש 4,5
בר 19,106a
ברא (1) 10,39
ברא (2) 30,159
ברד 28,90
בָּרָד 28,90a
ברה 26,19
ברוש 40,25
ברזל 37, III E. 6
ברח 9,8
בריא 30,159a
בריח 9,8a
ברית 26,19a
בֵּרֵךְ (1) 29,98
ברך (2) 4,6
בֶּרֶךְ 29,98a
בְּרָכָה 4,6a
בְּרֵכָה 40,44
ברק 29,115
בָּרָק 29,115a
ברר 19,106
בְּשֵׁם, בֹּשֶׂם 39,66
בשר 17,48
בָּשָׂר 36, III C. 7
בשל 15,140

בשת 5,3a
בַּת (1) 4,4b
בַּת (2) 41,117
בתולה 37, III E. 7
בתולים 37, III E. 7a

ג

גאה 27,65
גֵּאֶה 28,65c
גאוה 28,65b
גאון 27,65a
גָּאַל (1) 6,8
גאל (2) 20,195
גאלה 6,8a
גב 40,84
גבה 13,89
גֹּבַהּ 13,89a
גֵּבֶה 13,89b
גבול 26,20a
גבור 11,10a
גבורה 11,10c
גביע 41,118
גבירה, גברת 11,10d
גבל 26,20
גבעה 37, III F. 9
גבר 11,10
גֶּבֶר 11,10b
גג 39,56
גד 43,38
גדד 28,80
גדוד 28,80a
גדול 6,9a
גדולה 6,9d
גדי 40,45
גדל 6,9
גָּדֵל 6,9c
גֹּדַע 18,69
גדר 20,167
גֶּדֶר, גָּדֵר 20,167a
גדרה 20,167b
גוי 35, III B. 3
גויה 40,85
גולה 6,11a
גוע 17,49
גּור (1) 6,10
גּור (3) 21,196

גּוֹרָל	37, III E. 8
גָּז	20,151
גָּזִית	41,105
גָּזַל	14,131
גָּזַר	20,183
גַּחַל, גֶּחָל, גַּחֶלֶת	40,46
גַּיְא, גֵּיא	39,10
גִּיל	13,53
גִּיל	13,53a
גַּל	17,30b
גַּלְגַּל	17,30f
גֻּלְגֹּלֶת	17,30e
גָּלָה	6,11
גָּלָה	17,30d
גִּלּוּלִים	17,30a
גָּלוּת	6,11b
גָּלַח	18,61
גָּלַל	17,30
גִּלְעָד	43,23
גַּם	35,15
גְּמוּל	18,62a
גָּמַל	18,62
גָּמָל	37, III F. 20
גַּן, גַּנָּה	27,52b
גָּנַב	13,86
גַּנָּב	13,86a
גָּנַן	27,52
גָּעַל	21,220
גָּעַר	20,152
גְּעָרָה	20,152a
גָּעַשׁ	21,221
גֶּפֶן	37, III F. 18
גֵּר	6,10a
גֵּרָה	20,153
גֹּרֶן	38,49
גָּרַע	18,70
גֵּרֵשׁ	11,11
גֶּשֶׁם	28,76
גֶּשֶׁם	28,76a

ד

דֹּב	30,164a
דָּבַב	30,164
דִּבָּה	30,164b
דְּבִיר	3,4b
דָּבַק	10,35
דָּבָר (1)	26,21
דָּבָר (2)	3,4
דָּבָר	3,4a
דִּבֶּר	26,21b
דְּבַשׁ	37, III F. 21
דָּג, דָּגָה	38,44
דֶּגֶל	30,151
דֶּגֶל	30,151a
דָּגָן	38, III G. 24
דּוֹד	37, III F. 12
דּוֹד	43,2
דּוֹר	26,27
דּוֹר	26,27a
דּוּשׁ	19,142
דָּחָה	21,222
דַּי	38,26
דִּין	12,22
דִּין	12,22d
דָּכָא	19,115
דַּל	28,67a
דָּלַל	28,67
דֶּלֶת	37, III E. 9
דָּם	35, III B. 4
דָּמָה (1)	14,124
דָּמָה (2)	20,168
דְּמוּת	14,124a
דָּמַם	14,132
דֶּמַע	29,105
דִּמְעָה	29,105a
דָּן	12,22a
דָּנִיֵּאל	43,33
דַּעַת	3,7a
דַּק	20,169a
דָּקַק	20,169
דָּקַר	21,206
דָּרוֹם	40,47
דָּרַשׁ	6,12
דֶּשֶׁא	30,152
דֶּשֶׁא	30,152a
דָּשֵׁן	20,154
דֶּשֶׁן	20,154a
דָּת	39,19

ה

הֶבֶל	27,40
הֶבֶל	27,40a
הָגָה	15,158
הָדַף	21,207
הָדָר	28,86
הָדַר	28,86a
הוּא	35,16
הוֹד	6,21b
הָיָה	29,128
הָיָה	29,128a
הוֹי	38,6
הוֹם	31,165
הוֹן	29,95
הוֹן	29,95a
הִיא	35,17
הָיָה	3,5
הֵיכָל	37, III E. 10
הִין	39,11
הָלְאָה	40,54
הָלַךְ	3,6
הָלַל	6,13
הָלַם	41,106
הֵם, הֵמָּה	35,18
הֵמָּה	11,12
הָמוֹן	11,12a
הֵן	36, III D. 8
הִנֵּה	35, III B. 5
הִנֵּה	38,21
הָפַךְ	8,3
הַר	35,19
הָרַג	6,14
הָרָה	13,62
הָרָה	13,62a
הֶרֶס	13,63

ו

וָו	40,86

ז

זֶבַח	6,15
זֶבַח	6,15b
זֵד	20,184a
זָדוֹן	20,184b
זֶה, זֹאת	35,20
זָהָב	26,16a
זָהַר	18,71
זוּב	13,72
זוּל	30,138
זוּלָה	30,138a
זִיד	20,184
זַיִת	38,29
זֹךְ	31,173a
זֹכְךָ	31,173
זָכַר	4,7
זֵכֶר	4,7b
זָכָר	37, III E. 11
זִכָּרוֹן	4,7a
זִמָּה	39,67
זָמַם	19,107
זָמַר	12,32
זָנָב	31,183
זָנָב	31,183a
זָנָה	8,4
זְנוּנִים	8,4b
זְנוּת	8,4c
זַעַם	18,72
זַעַם	18,72a
זָעַק	8,5
זְעָקָה	8,5a
זָקֵן	11,13
זָקֵן	11,13a
זָקָן	11,13b
זָרָה	13,73
זְרוֹעַ	37, III E. 12
זָרַח	16,19
זֶרַע	10,28
זֶרַע	10,28a
זָרַק	14,109

ח

חָבָא	13,90
חֶבֶל (2)	19,116
חֶבֶל (3)	20,185
חֶבֶל	38, III F. 24
חָבַק	20,186
חָבַר	15,141
חָבֵר	15,141a
חָבַשׁ	14,115
חַג	16,25a
חָגַג	16,25
חָגַר	13,56
חָדַל	10,23
חָדַר	28,72
חֶדֶר	28,72a
חָדָשׁ	16,8
חֹדֶשׁ	16,8a
חָדָשׁ	16,8b
חַוָּה	6,16

48

רָעֵב	16,16a	שָׂכִיר	17,43b	שְׁבוּעָה	7,57d	שָׂחַק	29,118
רָעֵב	16,16b	שָׂכַל	9,36	שָׁבוּת	12,33b	שָׂחַק	29,118a
רעה, רֹעֶה (1)	7,51	שֶׂכֶל, שֵׂכֶל	9,36a	שֶׁבַח	21,216	שַׁחַר	18,58
רעה (2)	26,36	שָׂכַר	17,43	שֵׁבֶט	37,28	שַׁחַר	18,58a
רָעָה	9,34a	שָׂכָר	17,43a	שְׁבִי, שִׁבְיָה	12,33a	שַׁחַת	7,59
רעיה	26,36b	שְׁלֹמֹה	40,60	שְׁבִיעִי	7,57c	שַׁחַת	29,108a
רעם	20,191	שְׂמֹאל	27,53	שִׁבֹּלֶת	40,69	שֹׁטֶה	39,74
רען	29,123	שְׂמֹאל	27,53a	שֶׁבַע	7,57	שֶׁטֶף	14,129
רענן	29,123a	שָׂמַח	7,52	שֶׁבַע	7,57a	שֹׁטֵר	29,101
רעע	9,34	שָׂמֵחַ	7,52b	שִׁבְעִים	7,57b	שֹׁטֵר	29,101a
רעש	15,136	שִׂמְחָה	7,52a	שׁבר (1)	7,58	שִׁיר	9,39
רַעַשׁ	15,136a	שִׂמְלָה	39,62	שׁבר (2)	18,95	שִׁיר	9,39a
רפא	9,5	שָׂנֵא	7,53	שֶׁבֶר, שֵׁבֶר (1)	7,58a	שִׁירָה	9,39b
רפאים	9,5b	שִׂנְאָה	7,53a	שֶׁבֶר (2)	18,95a	שִׁית	9,40
רפה	13,55	שָׂעִיר	27,56a	שַׁבָּת	9,37	שכב	5,32
רצה	10,30	שָׂעַר	27,56	שָׁבַת	9,37a	שִׁכּוֹר	18,68b
רצון	10,30a	שֵׂעָר	27,56b	שַׁבָּתוֹן	9,37b	שכח	7,60
רצח	13,45	שְׂעֹרָה	27,56c	שׁגג	29,125	שָׂכַל	18,59
רצץ	19,113	שָׂפָה	37,27	שְׁגָגָה	29,125a	שכם	9,7
רק	37,26	שֹׂק	38,4	שָׁגָה	18,96	שֶׁכֶם	9,7a
רקיע	19,138a	שֹׁר	26,17a	שֹׁד	10,25a	שָׁכַן	7,61
רקם	31,172	שֹׂרד	28,92	שַׁד	39,7	שָׁכֵן	8,61b
רקמה	31,172a	שָׂרִיד	28,92a	שֹׁדֵד	10,25	שכר	18,68
רקע	19,138	שָׂרַף	7,54	שָׁדַי	38,5	שֵׂכָר	18,68a
רשע	11,7	שְׂרֵפָה	7,54a	שֹׁהַם	41,111	שֹׁלֵג	29,121
רָשָׁע	11,7a	שֹׂרֵר	26,17	שׁוא	27,61	שֶׁלֶג	29,121a
רֶשַׁע, רשעה	11,7b	שָׂשׂוֹן	15,153a	שָׁוְא	27,61a	שָׁלוֹם	8,63a
רשת	4,14b			שׁוֹאָה	27,61b	שׁלח	4,26

ש

שֹׂאת	3,14d	שׁאב	19,114	שׁוב	4,25	שֻׁלְחָן	37, III E. 22
שְׂבָכָה	40,59	שׁאג	18,94	שָׁוָה	18,97	שָׁלִישׁ	26,18e
שֹׂבַע	9,35	שָׁאָה (1)	27,48	שׁוח	29,108	שְׁלִישִׁי	26,18b
שֶׂבַע	9,35a	שָׁאָה (2)	30,136	שׁוט	20,192	שָׁלַךְ	8,62
שֹׂגֵב	19,104	שָׁאוּל	7,55a	שׁוֹט	20,192a	שָׁלַל	16,23
שׁדי, שׂדה	36, III B. 15	שָׁאוֹל	27,48a	שׁול	41,112	שָׁלָל	16,23a
שֹׂה	38,13	שָׁאוֹן	30,136a	שׁוע	18,83	שָׁלֵם	8,63
שֹׂושׂ	15,153	שָׁאַל	7,55	שׁוֹעָה	18,83a	שֶׁלֶם	8,63c
שְׂחוֹק	14,108a	שְׁאֵלָה	7,55b	שׁוֹעֵר	36, III B. 17a	שָׁלֵם	8,63d
שָׂחַק	14,108	שָׁאַן	31,191	שׁוֹפָר	37, III E. 20	שְׁלֹמֹה	8,63b
שֹׂטֵן	29,97	שַׁאֲנָן	31,191a	שׁוֹק	29,126	שָׁלַף	15,163
שָׂטָן	29,97a	שָׁאַף	20,182	שׁוֹק	29,126a	שָׁלַשׁ	26,18
שֹׂיב	29,124	שָׁאַר	7,56	שׁוֹר	37, III E. 21	שָׁלֹשׁ, שלשה	26,18a
שׂיבה	29,124a	שְׁאָר	7,56b	שׁוֹשַׁן	40,52	שִׁלְשׁוֹם	26,18d
שֹׂיחַ	19,105	שְׁאֵר	40,61	שֹׁזֵר	18,84	שִׁלְשִׁים	26,18c
שִׂיחַ	19,105a	שְׁאֵרִית	7,56a	שֹׁחֵד	29,109	שֵׁם	35,32
שֹׂים	4,24	שָׁבָה	12,33	שֹׁחֹד	29,109a	שָׁם	35,33
		שָׁבוּעַ	7,57e	שׁחט	9,38	שׁמד	9,41
				שְׁחִין	41,94	שָׁמָּה	9,42b